ACE YOUR MATH AND MEASURING SCIENCE PROJECT

Titles in the
ACE YOUR PHYSICS SCIENCE PROJECT series:

**Ace Your Forces and Motion
Science Project:
Great Science Fair Ideas**

ISBN-13: 978-0-7660-3222-4
ISBN-10:   0-7660-3222-1

**Ace Your Math and Measuring
Science Project:
Great Science Fair Ideas**

ISBN-13: 978-0-7660-3224-8
ISBN-10:   0-7660-3224-8

**Ace Your Physical Science Project:
Great Science Fair Ideas**

ISBN-13: 978-0-7660-3225-5
ISBN-10:   0-7660-3225-6

**Ace Your Sports Science Project:
Great Science Fair Ideas**

ISBN-13: 978-0-7660-3229-3
ISBN-10:   0-7660-3229-9

**Ace Your Weather Science Project:
Great Science Fair Ideas**

ISBN-13: 978-0-7660-3223-1
ISBN-10:   0-7660-3223-X

ACE YOUR PHYSICS SCIENCE PROJECT

ACE YOUR MATH AND MEASURING SCIENCE PROJECT

Robert Gardner

GREAT SCIENCE FAIR IDEAS

Enslow Publishers, Inc.
40 Industrial Road
Box 398
Berkeley Heights, NJ 07922
USA

http://www.enslow.com

Library of Congress Cataloging-in-Publication Data

Gardner, Robert, 1929–
Ace your math and measuring science project : great science fair ideas / Robert Gardner.
    p. cm. — (Ace your physics science project)
    Includes bibliographical references and index.
    Summary: "Presents several science projects and science fair ideas using math
      and measuring"—Provided by publisher.
    ISBN-13: 978-0-7660-3224-8
    ISBN-10: 0-7660-3224-8
    1. Metrology—Juvenile literature. 2. Science projects—Juvenile literature.
      3. Science fairs—Juvenile literature. I. Title.
    QC90.6.G37 2010
    530.8078—dc22

                                       2008023926
Printed in the United States of America

10 9 8 7 6 5 4 3 2 1

To Our Readers: We have done our best to make sure all Internet Addresses in this book were active and appropriate when we went to press. However, the author and the publisher have no control over and assume no liability for the material available on those Internet sites or on other Web sites they may link to. Any comments or suggestions can be sent by e-mail to comments@enslow.com or to the address on the back cover.

♻ Enslow Publishers, Inc., is committed to printing our books on recycled paper. The paper in every book contains 10% to 30% post-consumer waste (PCW). The cover board on the outside of each book contains 100% PCW. Our goal is to do our part to help young people and the environment too!

The experiments in this book are a collection of the author's best experiments, which were previously published by Enslow Publishers, Inc., in *Bicycle Science Projects: Physics on Wheels*, *Science Project Ideas About Rain*, *Science Projects About Math* and *Science Projects About Methods of Measuring*.

Illustration Credits: Stephen F. Delisle, Figures 1, 2, 3, 8, 9, 10, 11, 12, 13, 14, 15, 16, 17, 21, 22, 23, 24, 25; Michelle St. Germain, Figures 4, 5, 6, 7, 18, 19, 20; Jacob Katari, Figures 26, 27.

Photo Credits: Franck Boston/istockphoto.com, p. 56; Oleg Prikhodko/istockphoto.com, p. 78; NASA, p. 100; Shutterstock, pp. 3, 12, 34.

Cover Photos: Shutterstock

CONTENTS

🟡 *Indicates experiments that offer ideas for science fair projects.*

◔ *Indicates experiments that offer ideas for science fair projects.*

INTRODUCTION

When you hear the word *science*, do you think of a person in a white lab coat surrounded by beakers of bubbling liquids, specialized lab equipment, and computers? What exactly is science? Maybe you think science is only a subject you learn in school. Science is much more than this.

Science studies the things that are all around you, every day. No matter where you are or what you are doing, scientific principles are at work. You don't need special materials or equipment, or even a white lab coat, to be a scientist. Materials commonly found in your home, at school, or at a local store will allow you to become a scientist and pursue an area of interest. By making careful observations and asking questions about how things work, you can begin to design experiments to investigate a variety of questions. You can do science. You probably already have but just didn't know it!

Perhaps you are reading this book because you are looking for an idea for a science fair project for school, or maybe you are just hoping to find something fun to do on a rainy day. This book will give you an opportunity to learn more about math and to make many kinds of measurements. Science is based on measurements, and if you want to do science, you need to know how to measure things. You also need to be familiar with the units of measurement that scientists use. This book introduces you to math and measuring through experiments that are enjoyable to do. It will explore topics like early methods of measuring, the U.S. customary system of measurements, the metric system, and the Pythagorean theorem. It will provide opportunities to measure area, volume, mass, density, and temperature. If you are interested in making indirect measurements or estimates, there is sure to be something to catch your interest in the last chapter. You will learn scientific principles that will help you expand your understanding of both math and science.

THE SCIENTIFIC METHOD

All scientists look at the world and try to understand how things work. They make careful observations and conduct research about a question. Different areas of science use different approaches. Depending on the phenomenon being investigated, one method is likely to be more appropriate than another. For example, a scientist designing a new medication for heart disease would require a vastly different method than one studying the spread of an invasive plant species such as purple loosestrife or exploring whether there was once water on Mars.

Despite the differences, however, all scientists use a similar general approach to experiments. This approach is called the scientific method. In most experiments, some or all of the following steps are used: making observations, formulating a question, making a hypothesis (an answer to the question), predicting (making an if-then statement), designing and conducting an experiment, analyzing results and drawing conclusions, and accepting or rejecting the hypothesis. Scientists then share their findings with others by writing articles that are published in journals. After—and only after—a hypothesis has repeatedly been supported by experiments can it be considered a theory.

You might be wondering how to start an experiment. When you observe something in the world, you may become curious and think of a question. Often, your question can be answered by a well-designed investigation. Your question may also arise from an earlier experiment or from background reading. Once you have a question, you should make a hypothesis, which is a possible answer to the question (what you think will happen). Once you have a hypothesis, it is time to design an experiment. In most cases, it is appropriate to do a controlled experiment. This means you use two groups and treat them exactly the same except for the single factor that you are testing. That factor is called a variable. For example, if you want to investigate whether adding salt to water affects the time it takes the water to boil, two groups should be used. One group is called the control group and the other is called the experimental group. The two groups should be treated exactly the same: The same amount of water should be used, the water should be heated in the same way, and so forth. However, the variable—salt—will be different. The control group will contain pure water while the experimental group will contain saltwater. The variable is the only difference between the two groups.

During the experiment, you will collect data. For example, you might record the temperature of the liquid each minute, then note the temperature and time at which the liquid begins to boil. You might make observations of each liquid along the way. By comparing the data collected from the control group with the data collected from the experimental group, you will draw conclusions. Since the water samples were tested under the exact same conditions with the exception of the addition of the salt to the water, boiling of the saltwater at a higher temperature would allow you to conclude with confidence that this is the result of the salt being added to the water.

Two other terms that are often used in scientific experiments are *dependent* and *independent* variables. One dependent variable in the example is the boiling temperature of the liquid, because, in this case, it depends upon whether or not salt was added. The addition of salt is the independent variable (it doesn't depend on anything). After the data is collected, it is analyzed to see whether the hypothesis was supported or not. Often, the results of one experiment will lead you to a related question, or they may send you off in a different direction. Whatever the results, there is something to be learned from all scientific experiments.

SCIENCE FAIRS

Many of the experiments in this book may be appropriate for science fair projects. Experiments marked with a symbol (⬤) include a section called Science Fair Project Ideas. The ideas in this section will provide suggestions to help you develop your own original science fair project. However, judges at such fairs do not reward projects or experiments that are simply copied from a book. For example, models of geometric solids (cones, cylinders, cubes, spheres) and their surface areas or volumes would probably not impress judges unless they were done in a novel or creative way. On the other hand, a carefully performed experiment to determine how the surface area of an object affects the rate at which it loses heat would be likely to receive careful consideration.

Science fair judges tend to reward creative thought and imagination. It helps if you are really interested in your project. Take the time to choose a topic that really appeals to you. Consider, too, your own ability and the cost of materials. Don't pursue a project that you can't afford.

If you decide to use a project found in this book for a science fair, look for ways to modify or extend it. This should not be difficult because you will probably find that as you do these projects, new ideas for experiments will come to mind. These new experiments could make excellent science fair projects, particularly because they spring from your own mind and are interesting to you.

If you decide to enter a science fair and have never done so before, you should read some of the books listed in the Further Reading section. The books that deal specifically with science fairs will provide plenty of helpful hints and lots of useful information that will enable you to avoid the pitfalls that sometimes plague first-time entrants. You will learn how to prepare appealing reports that include charts and graphs, how to set up and display your work, how to present your project, and how to relate to judges and visitors.

SAFETY FIRST

As with many activities, safety is important in science, and certain rules apply when conducting experiments. Some of the rules below may seem obvious to you, but each is important to follow.

1. Have **an adult** help you whenever the experiment advises.

2. Wear eye protection and closed-toe shoes (rather than sandals), and tie back long hair.

3. Don't eat or drink while doing experiments and never taste substances being used.

4. Avoid touching chemicals.

5. Keep flammable substances away from fire.

6. When doing these experiments, use only nonmercury thermometers, such as those filled with alcohol. The liquid in some thermometers is mercury. It is dangerous to breathe mercury vapor. If you have mercury thermometers, **ask an adult** to take them to a local mercury thermometer exchange location.

7. When using a microscope, always use indirect lighting when illuminating objects. Never use the microscope mirror to capture direct sunlight. Because the mirror concentrates light rays, you could permanently damage your eyes.

8. When riding a bike, always wear an approved bike helmet and closed toe shoes.

9. Do only those experiments that are described in the book or those that have been approved by **an adult**.

10. Never engage in horseplay or play practical jokes.

11. Before beginning, read through the entire experimental procedure to make sure you understand all instructions, and clear all extra items from your work space.

12. At the end of every activity, clean all materials used and put them away. Wash your hands thoroughly with soap and water.

Chapter 1

Measuring and Units of Measure

WITHOUT MEASUREMENTS AND MATHEMATICS THERE WOULD BE NO SCIENCE. Galileo, the father of modern science, likened the universe to a grand book. He wrote,

> The book cannot be understood unless one first learns to comprehend the language and read the letters in which it is composed. [The universe] is written in the language of mathematics, and its characters are triangles, circles, and other geometric figures without which it is humanly impossible to understand a single word of it; without these, one wanders about in a dark labyrinth.

Nineteenth-century English physicist Lord Kelvin (William Thomson) once said, "When you can measure what you are speaking about, and express it in numbers, you know something about it." He went on to say, "When you cannot measure it, when you cannot express it in numbers, your knowledge is of a meager and unsatisfactory kind."

All measurements must be in units to have meaning. To say that a person is 5.5 is meaningless. We would all ask, "Five-point-five what?" The numbers become much more meaningful when we say the person is 5.5 feet tall. We know immediately that he or she is 5 feet, 6 inches tall. Similarly, if a recipe calls for 2 flour, the cook immediately wants to know 2 what? Cups? Tablespoons? Liters? Pints?

An American automobile driver stopped for fuel in England. She was surprised when, after filling the car's tank with gasoline, the cost was far more than expected. The numbers beside the fuel pump read 0.60; consequently, the driver expected to spend about $6.00 to fill the tank with about 10 gallons of gasoline. When the tank was filled, the price meter read 24.00, and the fuel-dispensed meter read 40.00.

In most foreign countries, fuel is measured in liters, not gallons. One liter is about 1.06 quarts, and it takes 3.785 liters to equal one U.S. gallon. The driver had purchased 40 liters of fuel at £0.60 per liter, resulting in a total cost of £24.00. The cost in U.S. money was about $40. The English pound (£) was worth about $1.67 when the gasoline was purchased.

Although measurement is essential to science, the earliest measurements were not made by scientists. They were made by craftsmen who realized that they could not make things that fit well together without measuring. The need to measure is even mentioned in the Bible. God tells Noah to build an ark 300 cubits long, 50 cubits wide, and 30 cubits high.

1.1 The First Units of Measure

Materials:
- an adult
- a room you can measure
- pencil
- roll of wrapping paper
- tape
- people, including adults, siblings, and friends

The cubit is the length of a person's forearm, from the elbow to the tip of the middle finger. The world's first units of measure, such as cubits, were based on parts of the human body. Other body parts that were used as units of measure are listed below and shown in Figure 1.

- The *foot* was a unit equal to the length of a person's foot, from the heel to the end of the big toe. It was about 2/3 of a cubit.

- The *thumb* was the width of a person's thumb. It was assumed to be 1/12 the length of a foot. The length of the top segment of the index finger was another unit equal in length to the width of the thumb.

- The *span* was the distance between the tips of the thumb and little finger when a person's fingers were spread as much as possible. The span was considered to be 1/2 cubit.

- The *hand* was the width of the person's hand. It was assumed to be 1/2 span.

- The *yard* was the distance from a person's nose to the tip of the middle finger of his outstretched arm.

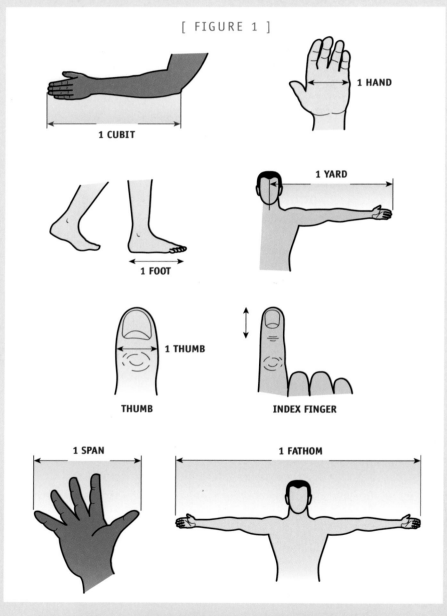

[FIGURE 1]

1 CUBIT

1 HAND

1 FOOT

1 YARD

1 THUMB

THUMB

INDEX FINGER

1 SPAN

1 FATHOM

The earliest units of measure were based on body parts.

- The *fathom* was two yards—the distance between the two middle fingers when a person's arms were outstretched.

Make a table to show the relationships among these various units of measure. For example:

1 fathom = 2 yards = 4 cubits = 6 feet = 8 spans = 16 hands = 72 thumbs
1 yard = ? = ? = ? . . .

Measure the length and width of a room in your house, using your foot as a unit of length. What is the length of the room in feet? What is the width of the room in feet?

Next, have **an adult** take the same measurements. How do your measurements of the room compare with the adult's measurements?

Use a pencil to mark the length of your cubit on a large sheet of wrapping paper. In the same way, mark the length of your foot, span, hand, and the width of your thumb. Tape a long sheet of the paper to a wall and mark the lengths of your yard and fathom.

Now determine whether or not your fathom is equal to two yards. Is your span equal to two hands? Is the length of the first segment of your index finger equal in length to the width of your thumb? Is your foot equal to 12 thumbs? Are two of your spans equal to your cubit? How does the length of your foot compare with the length of your cubit?

Compare the lengths of your cubit, foot, thumb, span, hand, yard, and fathom with those of other people. Include adults as well as siblings and friends. How do their units of measure compare with yours? What is the major problem in using body parts as units of measure?

Materials:
- paper clip
- long strip of thin cardboard
- pencil
- scissors

You can invent your own measuring system. Place a paper clip at one end of a long strip of thin cardboard, as shown in Figure 2a. Use a pencil to mark the length of the paper clip on the cardboard. You can give this length a name. You might call it a clip, or you can invent another name for it. Mark off nine more of these lengths end to end on the cardboard. Then use scissors to cut the cardboard so that it is exactly 10 paper clips long (see Figure 2b). Give this length, equal to 10 paper clips, another name. You might assign it your surname in your honor; you might call it a decaclip; you could name it with deca as a prefix to your surname; or call it *deca* plus whatever name you gave the length. *Deca* means "10 times," as in *decade* ("10 years").

Next, divide the smaller unit of length—the one equal to the length of a paper clip—into 10 equal divisions (see Figure 2c). Give these small units of length a name as well. You might use the prefix deci, which means "one tenth" (1/10 or 0.1).

Using the prefixes in Table 1, develop additional units that are multiples or fractions of the paper clip that you used as your basic unit of length. Which of these units can you actually mark on the ruler you have made or on others you could make?

Science Fair Project Ideas

- Design a system of measurement that uses the length of a coffee stirrer as its basic unit. Design another system that uses the width of a coffee stirrer as its basic unit.
- You know the meaning of such prefixes as *milli-, centi-, deci-, deca-, hecto-,* and *kilo-,* but what do the prefixes *mega-, giga-, tera-, micro-, nano-,* and *pico-* indicate?

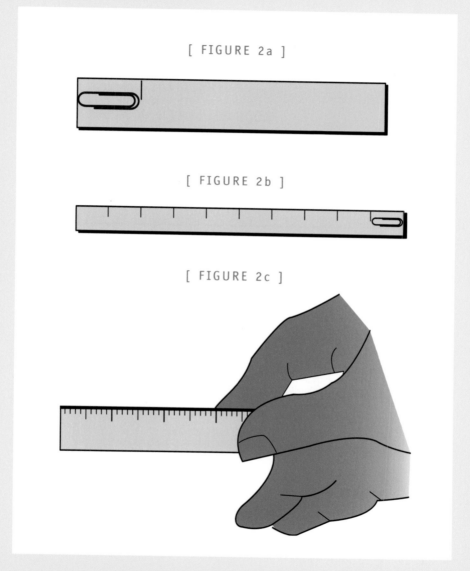

[FIGURE 2a]

[FIGURE 2b]

[FIGURE 2c]

2a) Mark the length of a paper clip on a cardboard strip. b) Repeat the process nine more times to make a length 10 paper clips long. c) Divide the paper clip lengths into 10 equal parts (deciclips).

TABLE 1
Prefix Names and Numerical Equivalents

Prefix	Meaning
micro-	0.000 001 m (1/1,000,000)
milli-	0.001 (1/1,000)
centi-	0.01 (1/100)
deci-	0.10 (1/10)
deca-	10
hecto-	100
kilo-	1,000

STANDARD UNITS OF LENGTH

As you found in the previous experiment, units of measure based on body parts are not very useful. Your foot may be considerably shorter than an adult's and significantly longer than your little brother's or sister's. If you and an adult carpenter were to build a house, all of the boards the carpenter requests that you measure and cut based on your body measurements might be too short. On the other hand, all of the boards you request that the carpenter measures and cuts based on his measurements might be too long.

To avoid confusion and arguments in building and in the marketplace, Henry I (King of England, 1068–1135) introduced the world's first standard unit of measure. Henry had an iron bar cut that was equal in length to the distance from his nose to the end of his outstretched arm. The bar, called the *iron ulna*, became the standard length for one yard.

Copies of it could be made and used throughout the land. These copies eventually became the yardsticks so common in our homes. This standard length provided merchants and customers with an impartial and unchanging measure in matters related to length.

Later, another English king, Edward I, decreed that 1 yard would be equal to 3 feet. The foot, in turn, was divided into 12 equal segments. Each segment was defined as one inch. Consequently, a foot was the same length as 12 inches, and a yard was equal in length to 36 inches.

THE U.S. CUSTOMARY SYSTEM

The U.S. customary system of measurements had its origin in the old "body parts" system that was gradually standardized beginning with Henry I. It is most widely used in the United States. As you can see from Table 2, the units are not related to one another in any mathematically simple or logical way.

TABLE 2

The U.S. Customary System of Linear Measurements

1 yard = 3 feet = 36 inches
1 foot = 12 inches = 1/3 yard
1 inch = 1/12 foot = 1/36 yard
1 rod = 16.5 feet = 5.5 yards
1 mile = 5,280 feet = 1,760 yards

The mile is a unit that was developed by the Romans. It was a distance equal to that of 1,000 paces by marching soldiers. (*Mille* means "one thousand" in Latin.) Since a pace, two steps, is about 5 feet, a mile was 5,000 feet. Today a mile is 5,280 feet.

The nautical mile, which is used by ships and planes, is based on a natural unit—the size of the earth. A nautical mile is equal to 1 minute of arc (1/60 of a degree) along the equator. Because the equator encircles the earth, it encompasses 360 degrees of arc.

THE METRIC SYSTEM

Before the Revolution began in France in 1789, there were a number of different units of measure in that country, which led to confusion. Slowly, a new decimal system of weights and measures emerged. But, sometimes the overzealous government tried to establish reforms that the French people and the rest of the world refused to accept. For example, the government introduced a new calendar consisting of 12 months, each with 30 days. To account for the additional days needed for the earth to make one orbit around the sun, the year concluded with a 5- or 6-day holiday. Each month was divided into three 10-day weeks. Each day was divided into ten 100-minute hours, and each minute contained 100 seconds.

Although the calendar and time systems were mathematically logical, they made it difficult to communicate with the rest of the world. The calendar was in effect for 12 years, but the clock was never widely accepted.

The basic unit of length in the metric system is the meter (m). French scientists and mathematicians designed the meter, to within less than 0.025 percent, to be one ten-millionth of the distance from the North Pole to the equator. In 1889, a standard meter bar with an X-shaped crosspiece was made from an alloy of platinum and iridium. The distance between two lines engraved across the bar was used to establish the standard meter. Today the meter is more precisely defined as 1,650,763.73 wavelengths of a particular reddish-orange light emitted by an isotope (one kind of atom) of krypton.

Today's metric system is known as the International System of Units, or *Système International d'Unités*. It is more commonly referred to as SI in all languages, and it is managed by the International Bureau of Weights and

Measures, whose headquarters are in Sèvres, France. In the United States, where both U.S. customary units and metric are widely used, the National Bureau of Standards defines the yard as 3,600/3,937 m or 0.9144 m. See the Appendix for conversions between many other U.S. customary and metric units.

In addition to the meter, which is the world's standard length, SI also includes standard units for mass, time, temperature, electric current, light intensity, and amount of substance. You will encounter some of these units later in this book.

Table 3 gives the SI units of linear measure, which are based on the meter. As you can see, it is a decimal system. All the units are related to one another by a factor of 10 or 1/10 (0.1).

TABLE 3

The SI System of Linear Measurement

1 meter (m) = 10 decimeters (dm)*   **= 100 centimeters (cm)**   **= 1,000 millimeters (mm)**
1 dekameter (dam)* = 10 m   **1 hectometer (hm)* = 100 m**   **1 kilometer (km) = 1,000 m**
10 mm = 1 cm   **10 cm = 1 dm**   **10 dm = 1 m**
10 m = 1 dam   **10 dam = 1 hm**   **10 hm = 1 km**

*seldom used

Materials:

-sharp pencil
-1-foot clear plastic
  ruler marked
  with inches and
  centimeters

-paper
-various objects

-calculator
-meterstick or
  long stick and
  clear tape
-long piece of
  thin rope

If you are not familiar with SI (metric) units of length, a few minutes with a meterstick will help you to understand how simple and logical these units of measure are. If you do not have access to a meterstick, you can make one from a stick that is about 40 inches long. Place a 12-inch clear plastic ruler that also shows metric units (centimeter and millimeter divisions) on the stick. Use the ruler and a pencil with soft lead to mark the 0- and 30-cm lines on the stick. Then use the same ruler to mark off centimeter divisions from 30 cm up to 100 cm. The centimeter marks are the longer numbered lines on the ruler. You need not mark the millimeter divisions, because you can use clear tape to fix the clear plastic ruler to the stick to cover the first 30 centimeters of your meterstick. That 30-cm portion of the meterstick can be used to take measurements that require millimeters.

Examine your meterstick closely. Notice that there are 100 centimeters in one meter. *Centi* means "one hundredth," so a centimeter is 1/100 of a meter. Each centimeter is divided into 10 equal units called millimeters. *Milli* means "one thousandth," so a millimeter is 1/1,000 of a meter. As you can see, there are 1,000 millimeters in a meter. Ten centimeters constitute a decimeter. *Deci* means "one tenth," so a decimeter is 1/10 of a meter. There are 10 decimeters in a meter. If you used your meterstick to lay out a line 10 meters long, you would have a dekameter (*deka* means "ten"). If you laid 10 dekameter lengths end to end to make a length of 100 meters, you would have a hectometer (*hecto* means "one hundred"). And if you placed 10 hectometers end to end, you would have 10 times 100 meters or 1,000 meters, which is a kilometer (*kilo* means "one thousand").

Use your meterstick to measure a variety of objects such as this book; the length, width, and height of a room; your own height; and so on. To make use of millimeters, you could measure the width of a pencil or a piece of string.

Measure your height in centimeters or meters. If your height is 150 cm, what is your height in meters? In millimeters? In decimeters? Notice how easy it is to move from one SI unit to another. Think about how much more difficult it would be to convert the same height—59 inches—to feet, yards, and rods.

Use a long piece of thin rope or thick string to make a measuring tape with a length of 1 dekameter. You can tie short pieces of colored yarn to your measuring tape at one-meter intervals. Use your measuring tape and meterstick to find the length and width of a soccer field. What other lengths would it be convenient to measure with such a measuring tape? How many times would you have to place your measuring tape on the ground to measure a length of 1.0 hectometer? To measure a kilometer?

Save your measuring tape and meterstick for measurements you may want to take later.

Science Fair Project Ideas

- There are 60 minutes in each degree of arc.
  a) How long is the equator in nautical miles?
  b) A nautical mile is 1.152 miles. What is the earth's circumference as measured in miles?
- The earth's circumference is 40,000,000 m.
  a) What is the earth's circumference in kilometers? b) What distance, in kilometers, is covered by one degree of arc along the equator? What is that distance in meters? c) What distance is covered by 1 minute of arc? d) There are 60 seconds in each minute of arc. The NAVSTAR global positioning system (GPS), which is a navigational system that uses several satellites and atomic clocks to determine location, can establish an object's position to within one second of arc. To within how many meters can the GPS determine a position on the earth?
- Find out and explain how the NAVSTAR GPS works.

1.4 Comparing Standard Units of Measure

As you know, rulers are used to measure length in both U.S. customary and SI units. Most commonly, rulers are divided into 12 inches, or 30 centimeters, or into 6 inches, or 15 cm. Yardsticks, of course, are divided into 36 inches, and metersticks contain 100 cm. Each centimeter is divided into 10 millimeters, so there are 1,000 mm along the meterstick.

In most countries, all measurements are made in SI units. In the United States, however, both SI and the U.S. customary units are in use. Carpenters and other craftspeople usually use the customary units. Scientists and a growing number of other people use SI units. As a result, it is often necessary to convert SI units to U.S. customary units or vice versa.

To find out how to make such conversions, make two marks exactly 10 inches apart on a sheet of paper, as shown in Figure 3. Next, use a metric ruler to find the distance between the two marks in centimeters. You will find that the distance is 25.4 cm.

If 25.4 cm is equal in length to 10 inches, how many centimeters equal 1 inch? Using a calculator, find the length of a centimeter in inches. What do you find it to be? How many centimeters are equal to one yard? What is the length of a yard in meters? What is the length of a foot in meters? In centimeters? What is the length of a meter in feet? How many meters are there in one mile? How many kilometers are equal to a mile? What is the length of one kilometer in miles?

Test as many of these conversions as you can directly by using metric and U.S. customary rulers, a yardstick, and a meterstick. Do your measurements appear to confirm the conversions you calculated? How do your conversions compare with those found in the Appendix?

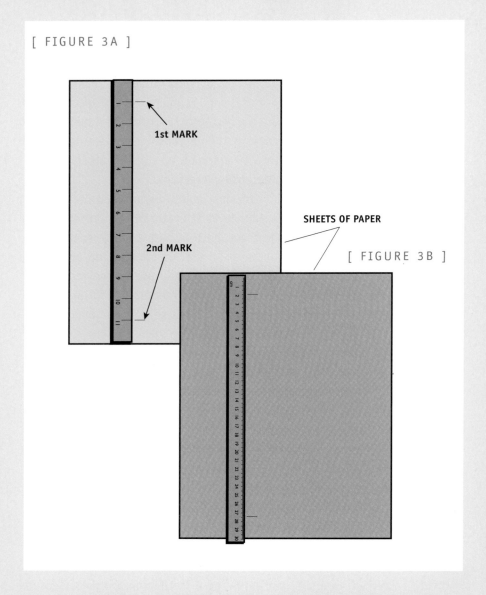

1st MARK

2nd MARK

SHEETS OF PAPER

[FIGURE 3B]

3a) Make two marks exactly 10 inches apart, as shown. Do not use the end of the ruler: it may be worn. b) Use a metric ruler to find the distance in centimeters between the two marks.

Science Fair Project Idea

In Experiment 1.2 you designed your own systems of measurement using paper clips or coffee stirrers as your basic unit of measure. Can you convert the units in the systems you designed into U.S. customary or SI units of measure?

Materials:
- pencil
- paper
- calculator

We sometimes have to convert units from SI to U.S. customary. Sometimes, we might have to do conversions within a system, from, say, kilometers to centimeters. This is easy to do if you use the factor-label method. This method involves using factors whose ratios are equal to one. As you know, multiplying by one does not change the value of a number, but it can change the units.

For example, if you want to convert 2.5 km to meters, you can multiply 2.5 km by 1,000 m/km. The value of 1,000 m/1 km is 1, because 1 km is equal to 1,000 m. The actual calculation would look like this:

$$2.5 \text{ km} \times \frac{1,000 \text{ m}}{1 \text{ km}} = 2,500 \text{ m}$$

We strike through the km units because km/km also equals one, so they cancel each other out. We have meters left, which is the unit we wanted. A unit divided by itself is 1, just as any value divided by itself is 1. For example, 2/2, 3/3, 4/4, and so on are all equal to 1; similarly, cm/cm, m/m, ft/ft, yd/yd are also equal to 1.

To convert 1.6 km to centimeters, you could do the following

$$1.6 \text{ km} \times \frac{1,000 \text{ m}}{1 \text{ km}} \times \frac{100 \text{ cm}}{1 \text{ m}} = 160,000 \text{ cm}$$

Both 1,000 m/1 km and 100 cm/1 m are equal to one, and the units km/km and m/m cancel out, leaving cm as the unit.

Converting from U.S. customary units to SI units or vice versa involves the same principle. For example, you have found that 2.54 cm is the same length as 1 inch. If you want to convert 15 inches to centimeters, the process is the same.

$$15 \text{ in} \times \frac{2.54 \text{ cm}}{1 \text{ in}} = 38.1 \text{ cm}$$

The value of 2.54 cm/1 in is 1 because 2.54 cm is the same length as 1 in, and the unit inch divided by the unit inch is also 1. (You might say the units cancel each other out.) That leaves centimeters as the unit for the number 38.1.

The factor-label method works both ways. If you want to convert 38.1 cm to inches, you would proceed in a similar way:

$$38.1 \text{ cm} \times \frac{1 \text{ in}}{2.54 \text{ cm}} = 15 \text{ in}$$

Or you could use the fact that one cm equals 0.3937 in and obtain the same result:

$$38.1 \text{ cm} \times \frac{0.3937 \text{ in}}{1 \text{ cm}} = 15 \text{ in}$$

The conversion factors in Table 4 will be useful when you have to change SI units to U.S. customary units or vice versa. SI units are predominant in this book because they are easier to use and because most scientific work uses SI units.

TABLE 4

Conversion Factors for U.S. Customary and SI Units

1.00 in = 2.54 cm
1.000 ft = 0.3048 m = 30.48 cm
1.000 yd = 0.9144 m
1.000 mi = 1.609 km
1.000 cm = 0.3937 in
1.000 m = 3.280 ft = 39.37 in
1.000 m = 1.094 yd
1.000 km = 0.6220 mi = 3282 ft = 1094 yd

Science Fair Project Ideas

- The length of a football field, excluding the goal areas, is 100 yards. Using the conversions in Table 4, calculate the length of a football field in meters. Then measure the field in meters. Does your measurement agree with your calculation?

- Devise a way to determine the thickness of a sheet of paper.

- At the equator, the earth's circumference is 40,000 kilometers. What is the circumference of the earth's line of latitude at 45 degrees north? At 60 degrees north? At the Arctic Circle? At the North Pole?

1.6 Body Parts and Ratios

Materials:

-ruler, meterstick, or yardstick

-people of different ages and genders

-pencil and paper

-calculator (optional)

-tape measure

In 1975, a team of anthropologists led by Mary Leakey found two sets of footprints that were 3.5 million years old embedded in volcanic ash near Laetoli, Tanzania. They had been made by feet that were human in appearance—the footprints of our ancestors. The prints of the larger individual, perhaps a male, were 21.5 cm (8.5 in) long and about 47.2 cm (18.6 in) apart; the other set were 18.5 cm (7.3 in) long and 38.7 cm (15.2 in) apart.

To determine the height of these upright creatures, the anthropologists assumed that a foot length is 15 percent (0.15) of an individual's height. What did they calculate the heights of these two creatures to be?

To see if their assumption was a reasonable one for present-day humans, you can conduct an experiment. Measure the foot length and the height of a number of different people. Try to include males and females of all ages. For each of the people you measure, determine the ratio of their foot length to their height. What is the average ratio of foot length to height for all the people you tested? Do your results for modern humans agree with the assumption made by the anthropologists about the human ancestors who made the footprints?

The ratio of foot length to height is but one of the many body-part ratios you might examine. Other ratios that you might try for a number of people include height to cubit, height to fathom, height to span, span to cubit, foot to cubit, length of small finger to length of nose, circumference of ankle to circumference of elbow, and any other body-part ratios you think may reveal a constant among a variety of people.

Do body-part ratios tend to be more or less constant among adults than among children?

Math and Science in Many Places

MATHEMATICS IS USED TO INVESTIGATE MANY THINGS.
In this chapter, you will explore great circles on the earth, properties of different varieties of apples, volume, mass, and density, as well as scaling, the golden ratio, and the effect of surface area on the rate of heat loss, all of which have a mathematical aspect.

2.1 Great Circles: Measuring on a Sphere and Scaling

Find Chicago and Beijing on a globe. What are the approximate latitudes of each of these two cities? An airplane flying from Chicago to Beijing will not fly along a line of latitude; its flight path is usually across the Arctic. To see why airplanes follow such a route, you will need some string and a meterstick or yardstick and the globe.

Calibrate the string by first putting it around the globe's equator. Place the length of string equal to the globe's equator on a meterstick or yardstick. What is the distance around the globe's equator in centimeters or inches? The actual distance around the earth's equator is 40,000 km (24,900 mi). Use this information and your measurement to find the globe's scale; that is, what distance on the globe is represented by 1.0 cm or 1.0 in.

Determine the distance from Chicago to Beijing on the globe if the distance is measured along a line of latitude. Use the same string to find the shortest distance from Chicago to Beijing. Record that distance. Why do airplanes fly over the Arctic when traveling between these two cities?

Use the string and globe to find the shortest flight paths between various cities that are far apart. Cars, trucks, and even oceangoing ships often do not follow the shortest routes along the earth's surface. Why?

The shortest paths between cities that you measured on the globe lie along what are called great circles. A great circle is a circle on the surface of a sphere where the center of that circle lies at the center of the sphere. Such a circle divides the globe into two equal hemispheres. Are any lines of latitude great circles? Which lines of longitude are great circles?

Materials:

- an adult
- several varieties of apples (about 6 apples of each variety)
- measuring tape, or a string and a meterstick or yardstick
- pencil and paper
- balance or scale
- clear cylindrical container (with a diameter greater than that of the largest apple)
- measuring cup and water
- masking tape
- marking pen
- long thin stick
- small aluminum pans (one for each variety of apple)
- knife
- oven
- pot holders

Buy a few apples of different varieties. Use a measuring tape to find the circumference, or distance around, each apple. If you do not have a measuring tape, use a string and a meterstick or yardstick as you did in the previous experiment to find the circumferences of the apples. What is the average circumference of each variety of apple? (The average circumference of one variety of apple would be the sum of the circumferences of all the apples of that variety divided by the number of apples in that variety.) Do the average circumferences of different varieties of apples differ?

Weigh each apple of each variety on a balance. Record the weights. Do the average weights of different varieties of apples differ? If they do, which variety is the heaviest? Which variety is the lightest?

To find the volumes of these same apples, you will need a clear cylindrical container with a diameter greater than that of the largest apple. You can convert the container to a graduated cylinder by measuring out known volumes of water and pouring them into the container. A piece of masking tape down the side of the cylinder will allow you to mark each volume of water added to the container with a line that has the proper number beside it (see Figure 4).

Empty the container. Pour a convenient volume of water into the cylinder and record the volume according to the marks you have made. Add an apple. Does the apple sink or float? What does this tell you about the apple's density?

If the apple floats, you can use a long thin stick to push the apple beneath the water. How much water does the apple displace? What is the apple's volume? Repeat this process for each apple. What is the average volume of each variety of apple? Do the average volumes of different apple varieties differ?

Taste each apple. Can you tell which kind of apple contains the largest percentage of water? Record the variety that you think holds the most water per gram of apple.

To test your prediction, you can measure the percentage of water in the apples by doing an experiment. Choose an apple from each of the varieties you purchased. Next, gather as many small aluminum pans as you have apples. On a piece of masking tape, write a number and the name of the apple variety you plan to place in the pan. Put the tape on the aluminum and weigh the pan. After you weigh the pan, place an apple in it and reweigh. Record the number of each pan as well as its weight with the apple in it. How can you find the weight of the apple alone?

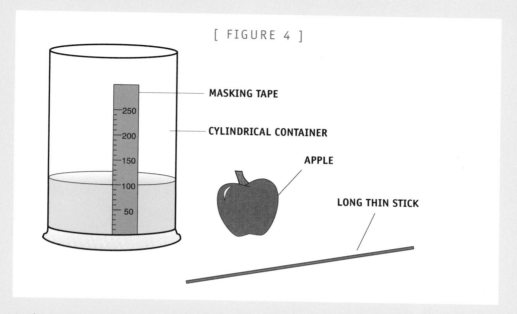

[FIGURE 4]

MASKING TAPE

CYLINDRICAL CONTAINER

APPLE

LONG THIN STICK

A clear, cylindrical container can be used to measure the volume of an apple. This container currently holds 100 ml of water. What will be the water level when the apple is submerged? How can you find the apple's volume?

Under adult supervision, cut each apple into thin slices in the pan. Place all the pans in an oven at 120°F and heat the apples for several hours. If your oven does not have a setting for 120°F, set the oven to Warm. The heat will make the apples dry faster.

Use pot holders to remove the pans from the oven. After the pans cool, reweigh each one. Repeat the process of heating and weighing until the apples show no further weight loss.

Calculate the weight loss of each apple. Since the change in the weight of each apple was due to loss of water, how much water did each apple lose? What percentage of each apple's original weight was water? Which variety of apple held the most water per gram of apple? (Be careful not to include the weight of the pan.) Was it the one you predicted? Which variety of apple held the least amount of water per gram?

Science Fair Project Ideas

- Try a similar experiment with popcorn. Weigh the popcorn before and after popping. Does the popcorn lose weight during popping? If so, what percentage of its weight does it lose? Do you think the weight of the popped popcorn will change if you dry it in an oven as you did the apples? Try it! What percentage of popcorn, by weight, is water?

- Which foods do you think contain very little water? Which foods do you think contain a high percentage of water? Test your predictions experimentally. What do you find?

Materials:
- beam balance or scale
- graduated cylinder or metric measuring cup
- standard masses
- cold water
- graph paper
- pencil
- ruler

How is the volume of a substance related to its mass or weight? In this experiment, you will be measuring mass. The mass of a substance can be found on a beam balance, which has a bar with a pan on either or both ends. Mass can also be found by using a scale. Any object placed on a beam balance will give the same reading everywhere. On the other hand, a spring balance measures weight. An object suspended from a spring balance will weigh more on earth than on the moon because the moon's gravity is weaker. Because the moon doesn't pull as hard on an object as the earth, the spring will be stretched less on the moon than on the earth. A beam balance gives the same reading on the moon as it does on the earth because gravity has the same effect on the pan on one side of the balance as it does on the other.

To find out how the mass of a substance is related to its volume, place a graduated cylinder or metric measuring cup on a pan on one side of a balance. Place standard masses on the other pan until the beam is balanced. Record the vessel's mass in grams. Add 100 ml of cold water to the cylinder and record its mass again. How can you find the mass of the water alone? Record the mass and volume of the water. Repeat the experiment for volumes of 80, 60, 40, and 20 ml of water.

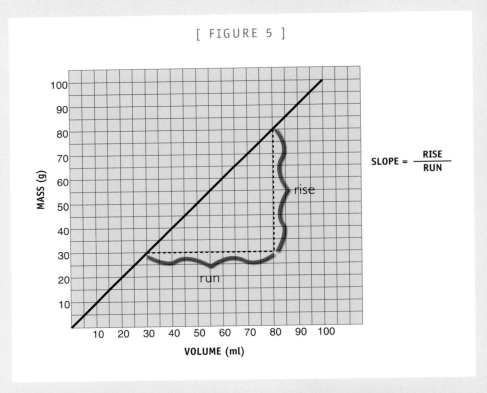

[FIGURE 5]

SLOPE = $\dfrac{\text{RISE}}{\text{RUN}}$

A graph of mass versus volume can be used to find the density of a substance.

Use the data you have collected to plot a graph by placing units of mass on the vertical axis, versus units of volume on the horizontal axis, as shown in Figure 5. Use a ruler to draw the best straight line you can through the points you have plotted. What is the slope (rise ÷ run) for this graph? Make several different measurements of the slope. Do all your measurements of the slope agree? What are the units of the slope: grams (g), milliliters (ml), grams per milliliters (g/ml), milliliters per gram (ml/g)?

As you discovered, the slope of the graph you made has units of g/ml because in finding the slope you divided mass, in grams, by volume, in milliliters. Furthermore, since the graph has the same slope everywhere, the ratio of mass to volume will be the same wherever you choose to measure the slope.

The slope of a graph of mass versus volume gives you the density of the substance on which the measurements were made. What is the density of water according to your graph?

A liter is equal to 1,000 milliliters (ml) or 1,000 cubic centimeters (cm^3). What is the density of water in grams per cubic centimeter (g/cm^3)? In grams per liter (g/l)?

Science Fair Project Ideas

- You might guess that different substances have different densities. To see if you are right, repeat the experiment using rubbing alcohol instead of water. What is the slope of this graph? What is the density of rubbing alcohol? Is it different from the density of water?

- As you have found, the density of a substance is the ratio of its mass to its volume. Graphs of mass versus volume for all substances will resemble those you made for water and alcohol. The slopes of these graphs show that the ratio of mass to volume is always the same for any given substance regardless of the amount measured. The value of that ratio (the density of the substance) is given by the slope of the graph and is different for most substances.

- To find the density of any object, all you have to do is measure its mass and its volume and divide the mass by the volume. To find the density of a solid with a regular shape, such as a cube or other parallelepiped (a six-faced figure), a cylinder, a cone, or a sphere, you can measure its dimensions, calculate its volume, and then find its mass on a balance.

- To find the density of an irregularly shaped object such as a lump of clay, first weigh the clay on a balance. Then roll the clay around a thread into a shape that will fit into a graduated cylinder or measuring cup. (Does changing the shape of the clay affect its mass?) Partially fill the graduated cylinder or measuring cup with water and record the volume of water in it. Lower the clay into the water until it is completely submerged. How can you find the volume of the clay from the change in the water level? How can you find the density of the clay? What is the clay's density in grams per milliliter (g/ml)? What is the density of clay in grams per cubic centimeter (g/cm^3)?

2.4 What Is the Effect of Surface Area on Heat Loss?

Materials:

- clay
- ruler
- 2 plastic cylindrical containers with about the same volume, one flattened cylinder (shaped like a pancake) and one tall cylinder
- alcohol thermometer
- clock or watch with a second hand
- graduated cylinder or metric measuring cup
- hot tap water (50°C or 120°F or hotter)

Use clay to make a cube that is 1.0 cm on a side. Based on what you found about the density of clay in the previous experiment, what is the mass of the cube?

As a first approximation, assume the cube of clay represents an animal. What is the animal's total (a) surface area? (b) volume? (c) mass?

Use clay to make a cube that is twice as wide, tall, and long. Again, let this cube represent an animal. What is this animal's total (a) surface area? (b) volume? (c) mass?

You have made two "animals." Compare them by finding the ratio of their (a) heights; (b) surface areas; (c) volumes; (d) masses.

As you have seen, the ratio of surface area to volume (or weight) is larger for a small body, such as a cube of clay 1.0 cm on a side, than for a large body, such as a cube of clay 2.0 cm on a side. The rate that heat is lost from a warm-blooded animal's body depends on its surface area. After all, it is the surface of the animal's body that is in contact with the cooler surroundings, be it air or water.

The relationship between the rate that heat is lost from a body and the body's surface area can be investigated experimentally. You will need two plastic cylindrical containers, one flattened cylinder (shaped like a pancake) and one tall cylinder. When these two containers holding equal volumes of water begin to lose heat, they do so at very different rates. In addition to the two cylinders with different shapes, you will need a graduated cylinder or metric measuring cup, an alcohol thermometer, hot water, and a clock or watch with a second hand.

Use the graduated cylinder or metric measuring cup to measure out 100 ml of tap water that is 50°C (120°F) or hotter. Pour the hot water into the pancake-shaped cylinder. When the water temperature reaches 40°C (105°F), measure how long it takes the water to cool to 35°C (95°F). Repeat the experiment using the same volume of hot water in the tall cylinder.

How much time was required for the water temperature in the pancake-shaped container to fall 5°C (or 10°F)? How much time was required for the water temperature in the tall container to fall 5°C (or 10°F)? Since heat loss in this case can be measured by the decrease in temperature, the rate at which heat is lost can be found by dividing the change in temperature by the time required for the temperature change to occur. In which container did the water lose heat faster? What is the rate of heat loss, in degrees per minute, for the water in each container?

To compare the surface area of the water in the two containers, pour 100 ml of water into both containers. Measure the diameter of each container and the depth of the water in it. Use your measurements to calculate the surface areas of the two samples of hot water in square centimeters (cm^2). (Figures 6a and 6b provide some useful information about surface areas and volumes for a number of different shapes. This information will be useful in other experiments as well.)

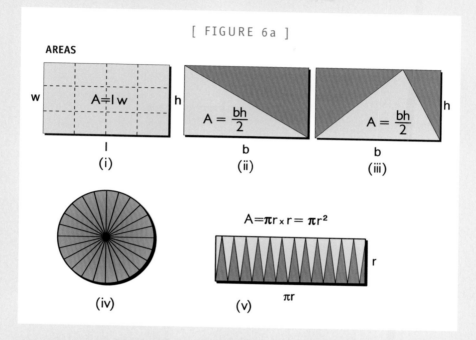

[FIGURE 6a]

AREAS

(i) $A = l \, w$

w, l

(ii) $A = \dfrac{bh}{2}$

h, b

(iii) $A = \dfrac{bh}{2}$

h, b

(iv)

(v) $A = \pi r \times r = \pi r^2$

r, πr

6a) Areas: Areas are measured in square units. A square 1.0 cm on a side has an area of 1.0 square centimeter (cm^2).

(*i*) The area of a rectangle *l* units long and *w* units wide has, as the drawing shows, an area of *l* × *w*. In the drawing, *l* is 4 units and *w* is 3 units. If the units are centimeters, the area is 12 cm^2.

(*ii*) A right triangle is half a rectangle so its area is ½ *bh*. Can you show that this same formula holds for the triangle in *iii* and, in fact, for all triangles?

(*iv*) A circle can be "sliced" into a large number of triangles with altitudes equal to the circle's radius and bases at the circumference so small that the curvature is negligible.

(*v*) When the triangles are put together in alternate fashion as shown, they form a rectangle with a height of *r* and a total base equal to half the circle's circumference or $\pi d/2 = \pi r$. The product of the rectangle's base and height gives the area of the circle: $\pi r \times r = \pi r^2$.

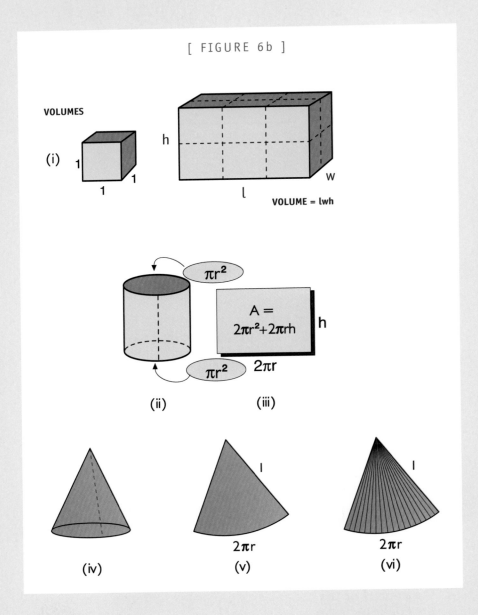

[FIGURE 6b]

6b) Volumes and areas of 3-dimensional objects:

(i) The basic unit of volume is a cube 1 unit wide, long, and high. If the units are centimeters, then its volume is 1 cm $\times$ 1 cm $\times$ 1 cm = 1 cm³. The parallelepiped shown is 3 units long, 2 units wide, and 2 units high. As you can see, its volume contains 12 basic units, which equals $l \times w \times h$. Its volume, therefore, is equal to the area of the base ($l \times w$) times the height. If the units are centimeters, then the volume is 3 cm $\times$ 2 cm $\times$ 2 cm = 12 cm³.

(ii,iii) The volume of a cylinder, like the volume of all regular solids, is equal to the area of the base $\times$ the height. Since the base of a cylinder is a circle, the volume of a cylinder is $\pi r^2 \times h$. The surface area of a cylinder is the area of top and bottom, $2 \times \pi r^2$, + the area of its round sides, which is πdh. To see where the πdh comes from, notice that if the sides of the cylinder are opened along the dotted line shown in *ii* and then flattened, they form a rectangle, as shown in *iii*, whose base is the circumference of the circular top and bottom of the cylinder, a length of πd or $2\pi r$, and whose altitude is the height of the cylinder, h. Thus, the total area of a cylinder is $2\pi r^2 + \pi dh$ or $2\pi r^2 + 2\pi rh$.

(iv, v, vi) A circular cone has a base with an area of πr^2. When opened along the dotted line shown in *iv* and flattened, the sides of the cone form a surface that can be thought of as a series of very narrow triangles with altitudes equal to l, the slant height of the cone. The total length of the bases of all the little triangles is the circumference of the cone's base, $2\pi r$. Since the area of each little triangle is equal to ½ its base times its altitude, the surface area of the cone's sides is ½($2\pi rl$). The total surface area of the cone is cone is $\pi r^2 + \pi rl$.

Can you show that the volume of a cone is $\frac{1}{3}\pi r^2 h$? Can you show that the volume of a sphere is $\frac{4}{3}\pi r^3$ and that its total surface area is $4\pi r^2$?

How did the ratio of the rate of heat flow from the two samples of hot water compare with the ratio of their surface areas? If they are nearly the same, then:

$$\frac{\text{surface area of pancake cylinder}}{\text{surface area of tall cylinder}} = \frac{\text{rate of heat loss from pancake cylinder}}{\text{rate of heat loss from tall cylinder}}$$

If this is the case, then you can conclude that the rate of heat loss is proportional to the surface area through which the heat flows. Of course, there are experimental errors and other factors such as differences in the thickness of the containers, so the ratios may not be identical. Experimental errors involve the unavoidable limits of accuracy in making measurements of length, mass, time, and volume. With better instruments, experimental errors are reduced.

How can you use your measurements of diameter and water depth for the two cylinders to confirm the fact that both cylinders contained 100 ml or 100 cm^3 of water?

2.5 The Golden Ratio

Materials:
-paper
-ruler
-protractor
-pencil
-calculator

-picture of the Parthenon
-pictures of buildings
-measuring tape
-a number of different people

Pythagoras was a Greek philosopher and mathematician who believed that all beauty and knowledge was to be found in numbers and their relationships. Musicians will tell you that the ratio of the frequencies of two notes, a topic first investigated by Pythagoras, determines whether they are harmonious. Early architects claimed that the key to beauty in architecture is the golden ratio.

The golden ratio, so named because objects with dimensions in this ratio were believed to have great beauty, was discovered through a geometric construction. You can discover the golden ratio for yourself by using a ruler, a protractor, and a sharp pencil to draw a square 10 cm on a side like the one shown in the scaled drawing in Figure 7a. Extend the base line WX to a point near the edge of the paper. Divide the square you have drawn into two equal rectangles, $UMNW$ and $MVXN$, as shown by the dotted line. Then use a compass to draw the arc of a circle with a radius equal to the diagonal of the rectangle $MVXN$ as shown in 7b. The arc should meet the extended base of the original square you drew. Next, construct a rectangle $VXYZ$ as shown in Figure 7c, whose base is the extended base of the square that intercepts the arc. Use the original height of the square as the height of the new rectangle.

The ratio of the height of the rectangle you just drew to its base ($VX \div XY$) is defined as the golden ratio, and the rectangle $VXYZ$ is a golden rectangle. According to your measurements, what is the golden ratio?

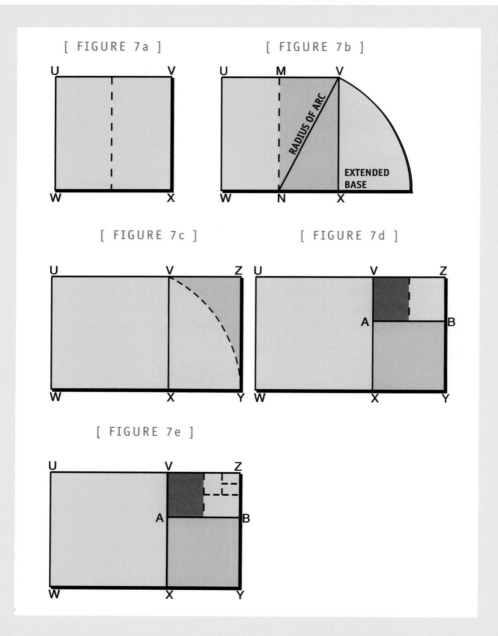

[FIGURE 7a]

[FIGURE 7b]

RADIUS OF ARC

EXTENDED BASE

[FIGURE 7c]

[FIGURE 7d]

[FIGURE 7e]

Constructions leading to the golden ratio and many golden rectangles

How closely does your value agree with the actual value, which is very close to 1.618, or about 8/5?

There are a number of reasons why Greek mathematicians and architects regarded the golden ratio with such reverence. The ratio of the length of the original square and its extended base, *WX* + *XY*, to the original base, *WX*, is the golden ratio. Furthermore, if you construct a square within a golden rectangle—*ABYX* in Figure 7d—the rectangle that remains, *ABZV*, is a golden rectangle. And a square constructed in that rectangle will leave a new smaller golden rectangle. The process can go on indefinitely, giving rise to smaller and smaller golden rectangles (Figure 7e).

Notice, too, if *WX* = 1.618 and *XY* = 1, then:

$$(1.618 + 1) \div 1.618 = 1.618.$$

Also, look at a series of numbers such that each number is the sum of the two preceding ones, as, for example:

1, 1, 2, 3, 5, 8, 13, 21, 34, 55 . . .

The golden ratio forms a series of numbers such that when raised to increasing powers, each term is the sum of the two preceding terms.

$$(1.618)^0, (1.618)^1, (1.618)^2, (1.618)^3, (1.618)^4, (1.618)^5 \ldots$$

Try it using the y^x key on a calculator. For example, to obtain 1.618^3, enter 1.618, press the y^x key, and then press 3, followed by the equal sign. You should find it produces a series that looks like this:

1, 1.618, 2.618, 4.236, 6.854, 11.09, . . .

Can you find any other number that works?

How about 1?

$$1^0, 1^1, 1^2, 1^3, 1^4, 1^5, \ldots$$

Clearly, 1 doesn't work because 1 raised to any power is 1. (Remember, any number raised to the 0 power is 1.)

Does the number 2 work? How about 3? Can you find any number other than the golden ratio that works?

If you've seen the Parthenon, which was built in Athens in the fifth century B.C., or pictures of it, you will find that it was built with the golden ratio in mind. Make some measurements of pictures of the Parthenon and other buildings or of buildings themselves. Can you find the golden ratio in the structure of any of these buildings? Do you find buildings with the golden ratio to be more attractive than square buildings or buildings with rectangles other than the golden rectangle?

Le Corbusier, a twentieth-century architect whose real name was Charles-Édouard Jeanneret (1887–1965), found the golden ratio in the structure of the human body. You can look for the ratio yourself. Begin by using a measuring tape to find the following lengths in a number of different people. Be sure to use the same units (centimeters or inches) in all of your measurements.

- Height
- Distance from floor to navel
- Distance from navel to top of head
- Length of upper arm
- Distance from tip of nose to tip of fingers when arm is fully outstretched to side
- Distance between tips of left-hand and right-hand fingers when both arms are outstretched
- Span (distance between tips of thumb and index finger of one outstretched hand)
- Distance from top of head to tip of fingers of arm raised straight upward
- Inseam (length of inside of leg)
- Cubit (elbow to tip of middle finger)
- Length of lower leg (knee to heel)
- Height minus Inseam

- Height minus Distance from floor to navel

- Distance from floor to tip of fingers of arm raised straight upward minus distance from floor to navel

- Distance from floor to navel minus Inseam

Look at the measurements you have made. Which ones can be paired to form ratios equal to, or very nearly equal to (± 0.2), the Golden Ratio? If the ratio of a pair of measurements is equal to the golden ratio for one person, is it equal or nearly equal for other people as well?

Chapter 3

Measuring Areas and Volumes

THE UNITS YOU READ ABOUT AND USED IN CHAPTER 1 TO MEASURE LENGTH, which has only one dimension, can be used to measure area and volume as well. Area is a measurement of surface. It has two dimensions, such as the length and width of this page. Volume is a measurement of the space occupied by something and has three dimensions, such as the length, width, and thickness of this book.

AREA

The area of the surface of this page is its length times its width. This may be written as an equation:

Area = length $\times$ width, or A = lw

To see why area is equal to length times width, think of the length, l, as a line that is "dragged" in a direction perpendicular to itself, as shown in Figure 8a. If it is dragged a distance w, it sweeps out a rectangle with a width w and a length l. Like all rectangles, it has four right angles (90-degree angles). If the length is 1 cm and the width is also 1 cm, as shown in Figure 8b, the surface will be a square. A square is a rectangle whose length and width are equal. The area within a square 1 cm on a side is said to be 1 square centimeter (1 cm^2). As you can see from Figure 8c, the number of square centimeters in any rectangle measured in centimeters is equal to its length times its width. In general, any rectangle with a length l and a width w encloses an area lw (Figure 8d). For example, a rectangle 6 cm long and 4 cm wide encloses an area of 24 cm^2 (6 cm $\times$ 4 cm). We write centimeters squared as cm^2 because, just as $2 \times 2 = 2^2$, so cm $\times$ cm = cm^2, inch $\times$ inch = inch^2, m $\times$ m = m^2, ft $\times$ ft = ft^2, and so on.

SIGNIFICANT FIGURES

When you multiply two numbers to find an area, your calculator may give you an answer that has more numbers than are necessary to include. For example, suppose you measure a large painting and find that it is 2.15 m long and 1.87 m wide. The fact that you write 2.15 m and 1.87 m indicates that you measured the length and width to the nearest centimeter, which is expressed as two decimal places. If you had measured to the nearest millimeter, you might have written 2.152 m and 1.870 m, because millimeters are expressed by three decimal places,. The readings 2.15 m and 1.87 m each have three significant figures. The last figure in each measurement, the 5 in 2.15 and the 7 in 1.87, are estimates. In making the measurements, you decided the last figure in measuring the length was closer to 5 cm than to 4 cm or 6 cm. You also decided that the last figure in the width was closer to 7 cm than to 6 cm or 8 cm. Any numbers written after the first number you estimated would be guesses rather than estimates.

Using a better measuring device, you were able to estimate the length to the nearest millimeter. You decided the last figure in your measurement of length was closer to 2 mm than to 1 mm or 3 mm, and that the last figure in the width was closer to 0 than to 9 mm or 1 mm.

Let's assume the 2.15-m and 1.87-m measurements are the best you can do. To indicate that you could measure these lengths only to three significant figures, you underline the last figure in each measurement and write 2.1<u>5</u> m and 1.8<u>7</u> m. Those last underlined figures are the first ones you had to estimate in making the measurements.

To find the area of the picture, you multiply the length by the width. Your calculator tells you that the area is 4.0205. You include the units m^2 because you know you are multiplying meters by meters. But, if you

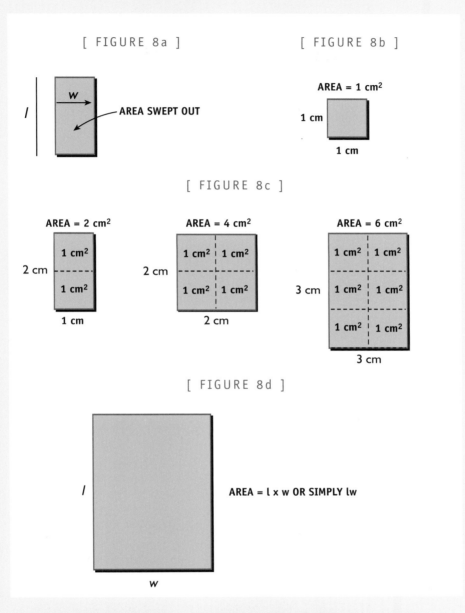

[FIGURE 8a]

[FIGURE 8b]

w

AREA SWEPT OUT

l

AREA = 1 cm^2

1 cm

1 cm

[FIGURE 8c]

AREA = 2 cm^2

1 cm^2

2 cm

1 cm^2

1 cm

AREA = 4 cm^2

1 cm^2 | 1 cm^2

2 cm

1 cm^2 | 1 cm^2

2 cm

AREA = 6 cm^2

1 cm^2 | 1 cm^2

3 cm

1 cm^2 | 1 cm^2

1 cm^2 | 1 cm^2

3 cm

[FIGURE 8d]

l

AREA = l x w OR SIMPLY lw

w

8a) Line l is "dragged" in a direction perpendicular to its length through a distance w. b) If l and w are both 1 cm, the area swept out is 1 square centimeter (cm^2). c) As you can see, the area within a square or rectangle is equal to the length times the width. d) For any rectangle with a length l and a width w the area it encloses is lw.

only knew each length to the nearest centimeter or hundredth of a meter, how can you know the area to the nearest ten-thousandth of a meter?

The answer is simple: You can't! The area should be expressed as 4.02 m². The area cannot have more significant figures than the least accurate measurement used to calculate it. The following equation shows why. The underlined numbers in the measurements are the ones you had to estimate, the ones of which you were unsure. In the example, any numbers that are the result of multiplication using an estimated number are also underlined. As you can see, the first digit in the answer that is uncertain, the one resulting from a column of digits containing a number based on an estimate, is in the third column. Consequently, the 2 in 4.0205 is underlined. Since it is the result of an addition involving an estimated measurement, all subsequent numbers are mere guesses. The answer should be rounded off to three significant figures, and the area should be written as 4.02 m².

$$
\begin{array}{r}
1.8\underline{7} \\
\times\ 2.1\underline{5} \\
\hline
9\underline{35} \\
18\underline{7} \\
37\underline{4} \\
\hline
4.0\underline{205}
\end{array}
$$

3.1 Area and Acres

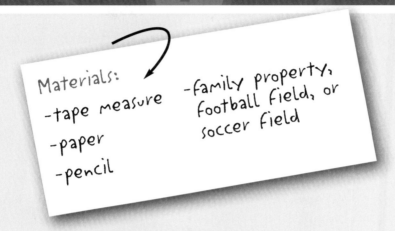

Materials:
-tape measure
-paper
-pencil
-family property,
football field, or
soccer field

In the United States, land area is measured in acres. An acre is an area equal to 160 square rods. A rod, as you may remember from Chapter 1, is 16.5 ft or 5.5 yd. How many square feet are there in an acre? How many square yards are there in an acre?

If your family owns the land where you live, use a tape measure to measure the boundary lines. Record the data and use them to draw a map of your family's property. Then calculate the area of the property in square feet. How many acres of property does your family own? If your family does not own the land where you live, measure the dimensions of a football field or a soccer field. How many acres are included within the boundary lines of a football field? Of a soccer field? What is the area of a baseball diamond in square feet? How many acres is this?

In most other countries, land area is measured in ares or hectares. An are is 100 m². A hectare is 100 ares or 10,000 m². How many acres are there in a hectare? In an are?

Convert the areas you measured in acres to hectares. Then use a meterstick and the 1-dekameter measuring tape you made in Experiment 1.3 to remeasure the land and/or fields you measured before. From your measurements in SI units, calculate the areas in hectares. Do they agree with the areas you calculated by converting U.S. customary units to SI units?

Science Fair Project Idea

If you were to paint your room, you would want to buy enough paint to cover the entire surface you plan to paint. Labels on paint cans indicate that one quart or one gallon will cover a certain number of square feet. How would you decide how much paint to buy?

3.2 Area of a Triangle

Materials:

- sharp pencil

- paper

You know that the area of a rectangle is equal to the product of its length and width. See if you can use this information to show that the area of a right triangle (a triangle with a 90° angle as shown in Figure 9a), is equal to ½ the base of the triangle times its height, or altitude.

Can you also show that this formula holds for any triangle, such as the one shown in Figure 9b? This is a more difficult task. However, if you extend the base of triangle *ABC* from *BC* to *BD* so that *D* lies directly under *A*, as shown in Figure 9c, you have another right triangle *ABD*. Now the task is to show that the area of triangle *ABC*, which is equal to the area of triangle *ABD* minus the area of triangle *ACD*, is equal to ½ *AD* × *BC*.

A trapezoid, (see Figure 9d), is a four-sided figure with only two parallel sides. Show that the area enclosed by a trapezoid is ½ the sum of the two parallel sides times the altitude, or ½(*b* + *d*)*h*.

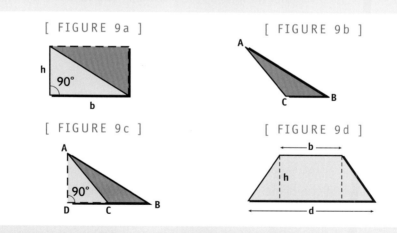

[FIGURE 9a]

[FIGURE 9b]

[FIGURE 9c]

[FIGURE 9d]

9a) Show that the area of a right triangle is equal to ½ its base times its height (½*bh*). b) Does the formula ½*bh* hold for all triangles such as *ABC*, or only for right triangles? c) Can you show that the area of triangle *ABC* is equal to ½ *BC* × *AD*? d) Can you show that the area of a trapezoid is given by ½ the sum of the bases × the altitude, or ½(*b* + *d*)*h*?

3.3 Circles: Their Diameters,

Materials:
-drawing compass
-pencil
-sheet of thin cardboard
-ruler
-scissors
-rubber tubing

The measured ratio of a circle's circumference to its diameter is nearly constant. In fact, if you measure very carefully, you will find that ratio is a constant that is approximately equal to 3.14. More precise measurements and mathematical theory reveal that the ratio is a never-ending decimal 3.14159 . . . , which is known as the Greek letter π (pi). Thus, the ratio of the circumference to the diameter is given by the equation

$$\textbf{circumference} = \pi, \textbf{ or } \frac{c}{d} = \pi$$
$$\textbf{diameter}$$

You can use this information to find a formula that will enable you to determine the area of any circle whose diameter or radius you can measure. (A circle's radius is half its diameter. It is the straight-line distance from the circle's center to its circumference.) Use a compass to draw a large circle on a sheet of thin cardboard, as shown in Figure 10a. With a pencil, mark the circle's center, which is where you placed the fixed point of the compass. Then use a pencil and ruler to draw a large number of closely spaced diameters across the circle (Figure 10b). With scissors, cut out the many narrow triangles into which you have divided the circle. The bases of all of these triangles are equal in length to the circumference of the circle, which is πd or $2\pi r$. (Of course, the bases of these "triangles" are slightly curved, but if you divided the circle into the tiniest possible sections, the bases would become straight.)

Arrange the triangles you have cut out as shown in Figure 10c to form a "rectangle". The width of this rectangle, as you can see, is the radius of the circle, r. Because half the triangles have their bases along the lower long side of the rectangle, the length of the rectangle is half the circumference, which is $\frac{1}{2}\pi d$ or πr.

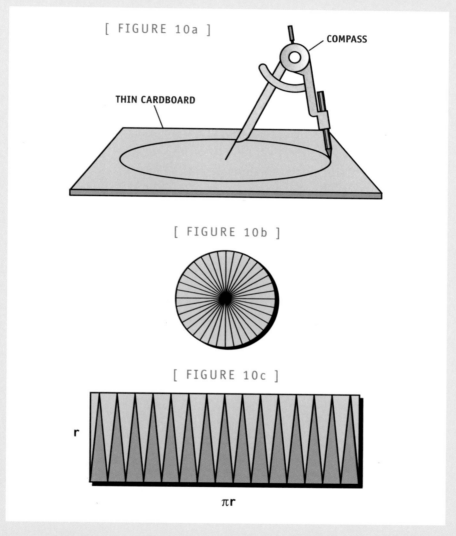

[FIGURE 10a]

COMPASS

THIN CARDBOARD

[FIGURE 10b]

[FIGURE 10c]

r

πr

10a) Draw a circle on a sheet of thin cardboard. b) Divide the circle into many small triangles, each with an altitude equal the radius of the circle, r. c) Cut out the triangles and arrange them in alternate fashion to form a rectangle. The rectangle will have a width equal to the radius of the circle, r, and a length equal to half the circle's circumference, πr.

Since the area of the circle has been transformed into a rectangle, you can find the area of the circle by finding the area of the rectangle whose dimensions are πr and r. What do you have to know about a circle to find its area?

Another way to find the area of a circle is to break it into a series of concentric rings, as shown in Figure 11a. These rings, which can be made from rubber tubing, can be straightened out and laid side by side to form a triangle (Figure 11b). How can you find the area of a circle, using this method? Does it agree with the formula for the area of a circle that you found when you cut the circle into a large number of triangles?

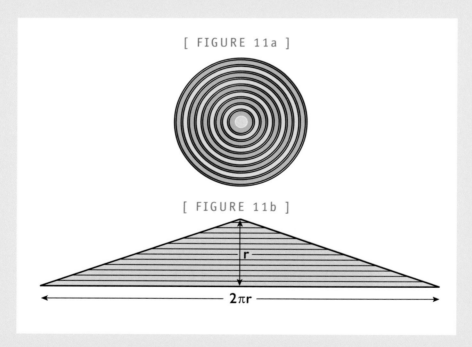

[FIGURE 11a]

[FIGURE 11b]

r

$2\pi r$

11a) A circle is broken into a series of concentric rings. Each ring can be represented by a length of rubber tubing. b) When the rings (tubes) are straightened out and placed side by side, they form a triangle with an altitude equal to the radius of the circle, *r*, and a base equal to the circumference of the circle, $2\pi r$.

VOLUME

Just as you dragged a line to sweep out an area, so you can drag an area to sweep out a volume (space). This is shown in Figures 12a and 12b. An area of 1 cm^2, if moved 1 cm in a direction perpendicular to that surface, will sweep out a cube 1 cm on a side, as shown in Figure 12b. A cube has a length, width, and height that are all equal.

The volume (space) of a cube that is 1 cm in length, width, and height is 1 cubic centimeter (1 cm^3). Again, it makes sense to label such a volume with the unit cm^3, because just as $2 \times 2 \times 2 = 2^3$, so cm $\times$ cm $\times$ cm = cm^3. If the dimensions of an object are 2 cm $\times$ 2 cm $\times$ 2 cm, its volume is 8 cm^3 (see Figure 12c). Show that the total surface area of such a block is 24 cm^2.

As shown in Figure 12d, the volume of any regular solid is given by the formula

Volume = area of base $\times$ height, or V = *lwh*.

If you rotate a rectangle or square around one of its edges while keeping that edge stationary, as shown in Figure 13a, you will sweep out a volume that is cylindrical. A hollow cylinder, such as a tin can, consists of two circular ends and a rectangle that has been bent to fit the circular ends (see Figure 13b).

If you rotate a right triangle around one of its sides while keeping that side stationary, as shown in Figure 13c, you sweep out a conical volume. What will be the shape of the volume swept out when a circle is rotated about its diameter, as shown in Figure 13d?

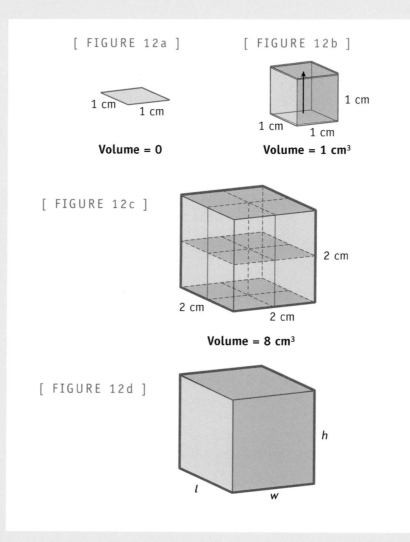

[FIGURE 12a]

1 cm 1 cm

Volume = 0

[FIGURE 12b]

1 cm

1 cm 1 cm

Volume = 1 cm³

[FIGURE 12c]

2 cm

2 cm

2 cm

Volume = 8 cm³

[FIGURE 12d]

h

l *w*

12a) If a square centimeter is "dragged" a distance of 1 cm in a direction
perpendicular to its surface, it will sweep out a volume (space) 1 cm
long, 1 cm wide, and 1 cm high. b) The volume swept out is 1 cubic
centimeter (cm³). c) The volume of an object 2 cm × 2 cm × 2 cm is,
as you can see, 8 cm³. d) In general, the volume of any cube or
rectangular solid is equal to length × width × height (*lwh*).

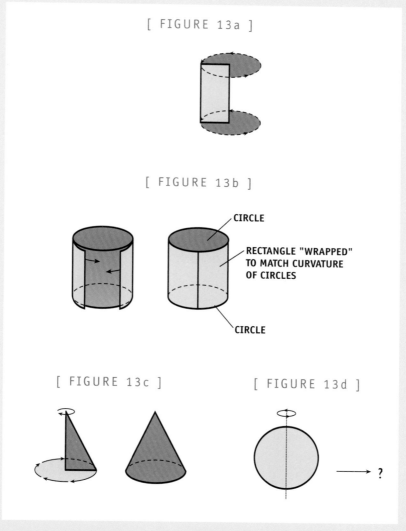

[FIGURE 13a]

[FIGURE 13b]

CIRCLE

RECTANGLE "WRAPPED"
TO MATCH CURVATURE
OF CIRCLES

CIRCLE

[FIGURE 13c]

[FIGURE 13d]

?

13a) A rectangle or square rotated about one edge generates a cylinder. b) A cylinder has two circular ends. The side of it is formed by a rectangle bent to match the curvature of its circular ends. c) Rotating a right triangle around one edge will generate a cone. d) What will be the shape of the volume swept out by a circle rotated about its diameter?

3.4 Cylinders: Their Area

Materials:
- cylindrical cardboard container (such as a salt or an oatmeal container)
- shears
- centimeter ruler
- water
- graduated cylinder or metric measuring cup
- basting syringe or funnel

As you found in Experiment 3.3, the area of a circle can be found by using the formula πr^2, where r is the radius of the circle. Since a cylinder is really a rectangle bent to fit the curvature of its circular top and bottom, you can easily work out a formula to find the surface area of a cylinder.

To help you arrive at such a formula, you will find it useful to take a cylindrical container apart. Remove the circular top and bottom of a cardboard cylinder such as a salt or an oatmeal container. Then cut the side of the container with household shears, as shown in Figure 14.

To flatten the side of the container, press it against the ground with your shoe. What is the shape of the side?

The total surface area of the cylinder consists of the two circular ends and the rectangular side that wraps around to form the curved side of the cylinder. Use the parts of the cylinder you have dissected to show that the total surface area of a cylinder is equal to $2\pi r^2 + 2\pi rh$, or $\frac{1}{2}\pi d^2 + \pi dh$, where r is the radius of the cylinder (or d is its diameter) and h is its height.

The volume of a regular solid is the area of its base times its height. In the case of a cylinder, the area of the base is πr^2. If the base of a hollow cylinder has a radius of 10 cm, the area of that base is $\pi \times (10 \text{ cm})^2$, or 314 cm^2. If water is poured into the cylinder to a depth of 1 cm, the volume of water in the cylinder should be 314 cm^3. If the depth of the water is 10 cm, its volume should be 3,140 cm^3. In general, the volume should be given by the formula $\pi r^2 h$, where πr^2 is the area of the base and h is the height of the cylinder or the fluid in it.

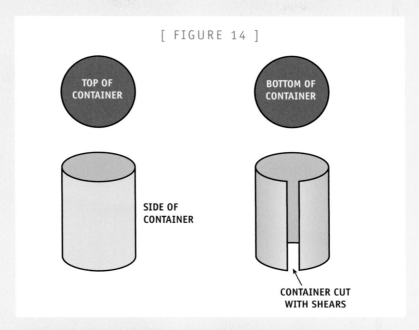

[FIGURE 14]

TOP OF
CONTAINER

BOTTOM OF
CONTAINER

SIDE OF
CONTAINER

CONTAINER CUT
WITH SHEARS

A cylindrical container can be dissected by removing the top and bottom, then cutting down through the side with shears.

The units are correct because a volume has three dimensions, and the units of a radius squared will be square units, such as cm^2. When multiplied by the height, h, the units become cubic. For example, cm^2 × cm = cm^3.

You can test this formula ($\pi r^2 h$) by using a centimeter ruler to measure the inside diameter and height of a can and then filling it with water. Using your measurements, predict the volume of water in the can. Then, pour the water into a graduated cylinder or metric measuring cup. If you have difficulty pouring the water from the can, you can use a basting syringe or a funnel to transfer the water to the graduated cylinder.

What was the volume of water in the can? (Do not be concerned if the graduated cylinder or measuring cup measures volume in milliliters [ml], because 1 ml is the same volume as 1 cm^3.) How closely does it agree with the volume you calculated using the formula?

Materials:
- paper and pencil
- ruler
- hollow cylinder (such as a frozen orange juice container)
- drawing compass
- heavy paper
- scissors
- tape
- marking pen
- salt or fine sand

The surface area of a cone consists of the circular base and the slanted sides. The area of the base is simply πr^2. The area of the side can be found by dividing that surface into a large number of tiny triangles, as shown in Figure 15a. If the triangles are alternately arranged to form a rectangle, as shown in Figure 15b, the rectangle will have a height equal to the slant height of the cone, s, and a base or length equal to ½ the circumference of the cone's base, or πr. Hence, the total surface area of the cone will be $\pi r^2 + \pi r s$.

You may also see the area of a cone expressed as

$$\pi r^2 + \pi r \sqrt{(r^2 + h^2)}.$$

This is because the slant height, s, is the hypotenuse of the right triangle hrs shown in Figure 15c. According to the Pythagorean theorem, the sum of the squares of the legs of any right triangle is equal to the square of the hypotenuse, also shown in Figure 15c. Since $s^2 = r^2 + h^2$, s is equal to the square root of $r^2 + h^2$.

To demonstrate for yourself that the Pythagorean theorem works, draw some right triangles. Some easy ones to test are right triangles with sides that are 3 units and 4 units, 6 units and 8 units, 9 units and 12 units, and 1.5 units and 2 units. Then measure the hypotenuses

[FIGURE 15a]

[FIGURE 15b]

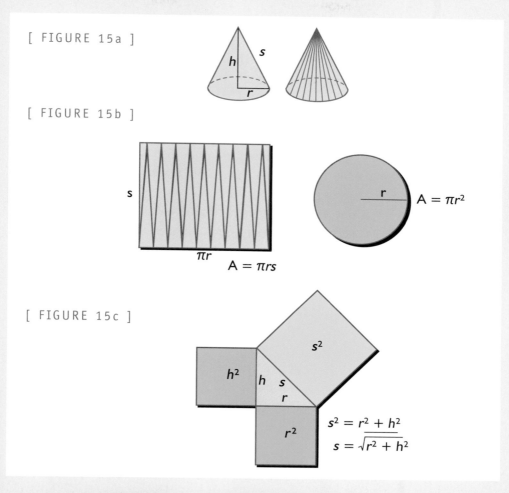

$$A = \pi r^2$$

$$A = \pi rs$$

[FIGURE 15c]

$$s^2 = r^2 + h^2$$

$$s = \sqrt{r^2 + h^2}$$

15a) A cone's surface area can be determined by dividing its side into many tiny triangles. b) When the triangles are arranged to form a rectangle, the height of the rectangle is s, the slant height of the cone. The length of the base of the rectangle is πr, or half the circumference of the cone's base, so the area of the rectangle is πrs. The area of the cone's base is πr^2. Thus the total surface area of the cone is $\pi r^2 + \pi rs$. c) The Pythagorean theorem tells us that $s^2 = r^2 + h^2$. Therefore, the cone's slant height, s, can be obtained from the square root of $r^2 + h^2$. Consequently, the cone's area may be expressed as $\pi r^2 + \pi r \sqrt{(r^2 + h^2)}$.

and square the lengths of all three sides. You will find that the sum of the squares of the legs equals the square of the hypotenuse.

The volume of a cone can be determined by an experiment. Find a hollow cylinder such as the kind that frozen orange juice comes in. Measure the inside diameter of the can. Then use a compass to draw a circle on heavy paper. The *radius* of the circle that you draw should be equal to the inside *diameter* of the cylinder. With scissors, cut out the circle and fold it along a diameter, as shown in Figure 16a. Cut the circle along that diameter. Take the half circle and form it into a cone, as shown in Figure 16b. Use tape to seal the seam along the cone's slant height.

Measure the diameter of the cone you have made. You will find it has the same diameter as the inside diameter of the cylinder. Can you explain why?

To find the height of the cone, place it next to the cylinder, as shown in Figure 16c. Use a marking pen to mark the height on the side of the cylinder, and measure that height with a ruler.

Another way to find the height is to measure the slant height. Since $s^2 = r^2 + h^2$, then $h^2 = s^2 - r^2$. Consequently, the height of the cone can be found from the square root of $s^2 - r^2$.

Mark the cone's height on the *inside* of the cylinder. Then fill the cone with salt or fine sand and pour it into the cylinder. You will find that emptying exactly 3 conefuls of the solid into the cylinder will fill it to the height you marked on the inside of the cylinder. Consequently, you know that the volume of a cone is one third that of a cylinder of the same diameter and height. Since the volume of a cylinder is given by the formula $\pi r^2 h$, the volume of a cone is $\frac{1}{3} \pi r^2 h$.

Science Fair Project Idea

Show that the cone you made in this experiment has the same circumference and diameter as the cylinder you used in the experiment.

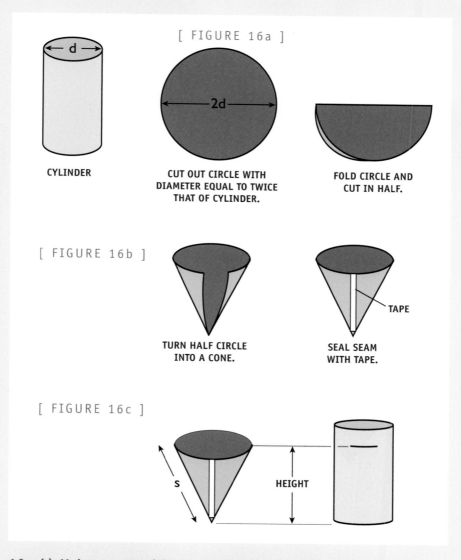

[FIGURE 16a]

CYLINDER

CUT OUT CIRCLE WITH
DIAMETER EQUAL TO TWICE
THAT OF CYLINDER.

FOLD CIRCLE AND
CUT IN HALF.

[FIGURE 16b]

TURN HALF CIRCLE
INTO A CONE.

SEAL SEAM
WITH TAPE.

TAPE

[FIGURE 16c]

s

HEIGHT

16a, b) Make a cone with the same diameter as a cylinder. Mark the cone's height on the cylinder. c) The cone's height can also be found from the slant height of the cone, s. Since $s^2 = r^2 + h^2$, $h^2 = s^2 - r^2$, and so $h = \sqrt{(s^2 - r^2)}$. Use your pocket calculator to find $\sqrt{(s^2 - r^2)}$.

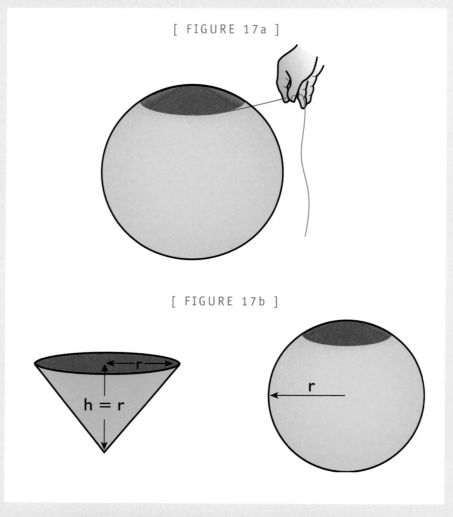

[FIGURE 17a]

[FIGURE 17b]

h = r

r

r

17a) By carefully winding string around a globe, you can find the area of a sphere. b) A cone with _h_ = _r_ and a sphere with same radius as the cone are shown here. Four conefuls are required to just fill the sphere. Since the cone's volume is given by $\frac{1}{3}\pi r^2 h$, or, since _h_ = _r_, by $\frac{1}{3}\pi r^3$, the sphere's volume is equal to $4 \times \frac{1}{3}\pi r^3$, or $\frac{4}{3}\pi r^3$.

THE SURFACE AREAS AND VOLUMES OF SPHERES

The surface area of a sphere is more difficult to derive. Since it is round, you can be sure π is involved, and because it is an area, r^2 will be part of the formula. One approach is to wrap string around the Northern Hemisphere of a globe, as shown in Figure 17a. From the number of windings and the length and width of the string, you can find the area of half the globe. If done carefully, you will find that the area of the string is equal to π times twice the globe's radius squared. This means that the total surface area of the globe is $4\pi r^2$.

The volume of a sphere can be determined in a way that is similar to the way you found the volume of a cone. Fill a hollow cone with a radius *and* height equal to the radius of a hollow sphere with water (see Figure 17b). The cone can be filled and emptied into the sphere exactly four times. At that point, the sphere will be completely filled. This tells you that the volume of a sphere is $4 \times \frac{1}{3}\pi r^3$, or $\frac{4}{3}\pi r^3$.

Chapter 4

Math, Temperature, and Heat

THIS CHAPTER FOCUSES ON THE MATHEMATICS RELATED TO MEASURING TEMPERATURE AND HEAT. You will investigate four different temperature scales. You are probably familiar with the Celsius and Fahrenheit scales, but the Kelvin and Rankine scales may be new to you. You will discover how mathematics is used to measure heat, how it enables us to find the heat needed to melt a gram of water (heat of fusion), boil away a gram of water (heat of vaporization), or determine the heat required to raise the temperature of one gram of any substance by one degree (specific heat).

Materials:
- graph paper
- pencil
- ruler
- Celsius and Fahrenheit scales

In most countries, weather reports give temperatures in degrees Celsius (°C). In the United States, temperatures are more often reported in degrees Fahrenheit (°F). How are these two scales related?

Both the Celsius and the Fahrenheit temperature scales are based on two fixed points—two temperatures that are determined by nature regardless of the scale used to measure them. These two fixed points are the temperature at which water freezes (or melts) and the temperature at which it boils (or condenses) when at atmospheric pressure. Atmospheric pressure is the pressure of the air at sea level (a barometer reading of 760 mm or 30 in of mercury).

On the Celsius scale, the freezing point of water is defined as 0°C; on the Fahrenheit scale, the same temperature is defined as 32°F. The temperature of boiling water on the Celsius scale is 100°C; on the Fahrenheit scale, it is 212°F.

Using these two fixed points, you can plot a graph like the one in Figure 18. It shows the temperature in degrees Fahrenheit along the vertical axis plotted against the corresponding temperatures in degrees Celsius along the horizontal axis. The two fixed points are indicated. On your graph, you can use the fixed points to draw a straight line that extends to at least –50°F on the lower end and to 300°F on the upper end.

Use your graph to find the temperature in degrees Fahrenheit when the temperature in degrees Celsius is (a) 0°C; (b) 20°C; (c) 45°C; (d) 120°C; (e) –10°C; (f) –40°C. Then use the same graph to find the temperature in degrees Celsius when the Fahrenheit temperature is (a) 212°F; (b) 40°F; (c) 100°F; (d) 290°F; (e) 0°F; (f) –40°F.

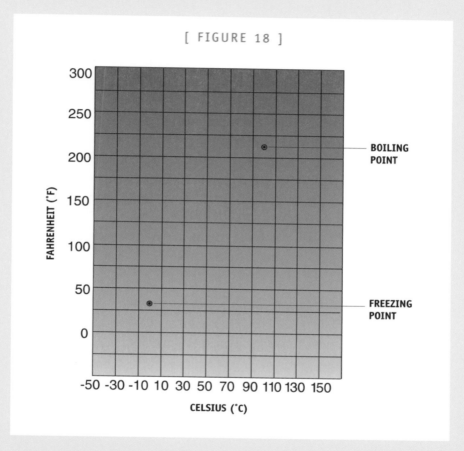

[FIGURE 18]

The freezing and boiling points of water serve as fixed temperatures on both the Celsius and Fahrenheit scales.

At what temperature do the two scales have the same numeric value?

You can write a formula that allows you to convert temperatures from one scale to the other. To begin, figure out the number of degrees between the freezing point and boiling point on each scale. How many degrees are there between these two fixed temperatures on the Fahrenheit scale? On the Celsius scale? How many degrees Fahrenheit are equal to one degree Celsius? How many degrees Celsius are equal to one degree Fahrenheit?

If the temperature on the Celsius scale is ten degrees above the freezing point, how many degrees is it above the freezing point on the Fahrenheit scale? Since the Fahrenheit scale begins not at 0° but at 32°, what number must be added to the number of Fahrenheit degrees above the freezing point to find the actual temperature in degrees Fahrenheit that corresponds to 10°C?

From what you have done, fill in the blanks in the equation below. This equation will allow you to convert temperatures from °C to °F.

$$°F = \underline{\quad} °C + \underline{\quad}$$

Does the equation work for negative temperatures?

See if you can find a similar equation that will allow you to convert Fahrenheit temperatures to Celsius temperatures.

CELSIUS AND KELVIN SCALES

During the mid-nineteenth century, William Thomson, who became Lord Kelvin later in life, introduced another temperature scale. Thomson discovered that the coldest possible temperature, the temperature at which molecules would stop moving, was −273°C. He called this temperature absolute zero, because lower temperatures were impossible. To avoid negative temperatures, he invented what he called the absolute temperature scale. Today that scale is known as the Kelvin scale in honor of Lord Kelvin.

On the Kelvin scale, degrees are referred to as kelvins, and −273°C is defined as 0 K, not 0°K. The value of a kelvin is the same as a degree on the Celsius scale; that is, the temperature range between the freezing and boiling points of water is 100 kelvins. Because 0 K is equal to −273°C and a kelvin has the same value as a degree Celsius, the freezing point of water is 273 K on the Kelvin scale. What is the boiling point of water on the Kelvin scale?

Plot a graph of temperature using degrees Celsius on the vertical axis and Kelvin temperatures on the horizontal axis. What is the temperature in degrees Celsius when the Kelvin temperature is (a) 0 K? (b) 273 K? (c) 373 K? (d) 323 K? (e) 423 K? (f) 100 K? What is the temperature in kelvins when the Celsius temperature is (a) 0°C? (b) −273°C? (c) 100°C? (d) 50°C? (e) 150°C? (f) −50°C?

Write an equation that allows you to convert any temperature on the Kelvin scale to degrees Celsius. Write another equation that allows you to convert temperatures on the Celsius scale to kelvins.

RANKINE AND FAHRENHEIT SCALES

William Rankine invented yet another temperature scale. His scale made use of Kelvin's absolute zero but used degrees equal in value to the degrees on the Fahrenheit scale. On the Rankine scale, the value of a degree Rankine is the same as a degree Fahrenheit, but 0°R is absolute zero.

 Science Fair Project Idea

Using what you have learned, write equations that allow you to convert (a) Fahrenheit to Rankine; (b) Rankine to Fahrenheit; (c) Rankine to kelvins; (d) Rankine to Celsius.

Materials:

- an adult

- Styrofoam cups, 6- or 7-oz and 12-oz

- glasses or beakers to hold Styrofoam cups

- cold water, about 10°C below room temperature

- graduated cylinder or metric measuring cup

- electric immersion heater

- alcohol thermometer with Celsius scale (−10°C to 110°C)

- electrical outlet

- stopwatch or clock or watch with second hand

- refrigerator

Because this experiment requires the use of household electricity, it should be done under adult supervision.

Heat is defined as the energy transferred between two substances because of a difference in their temperatures. Heat always "flows" from a warmer substance to a cooler one.

Early scientists believed that heat was an invisible, weightless fluid that flowed from warm bodies to cooler ones. That concept of heat persists today: We still speak of heat flowing from hot objects to cooler ones even though we know the transfer is accomplished by collisions between molecules.

Heat is measured in units called calories or joules. A calorie (cal) is the heat transferred when the temperature of one gram of water rises by one degree Celsius. A joule is the heat transferred when one gram of water rises by 0.24°C. For your work, the calorie is the easier unit to use.

In this experiment, you will measure the heat delivered per minute by an immersion heater. Because you will be using an electrical device submerged in water that you will connect to an electric outlet, you should **work under the supervision of a knowledgeable adult.**

Put a 6- or 7-oz Styrofoam cup in a glass or beaker. The glass will provide better support for the light, somewhat unstable Styrofoam. Pour 100 g of *cold* water into the Styrofoam cup. The water should be cold— about 10°C (18°F) below room temperature—because the water will lose heat to the cooler air when its temperature rises above that of the surrounding air. By starting with the water below the temperature of the room, some heat will flow into the water during the first part of the heating process. This will compensate for the heat lost when the water temperature exceeds room temperature.

It is not necessary to weigh the water. Since 1.0 ml of water weighs 1.0 g, you can obtain 100 g of water by pouring 100 ml of cold water into the Styrofoam cup.

Place the unconnected immersion heater in the water along with an alcohol thermometer, as shown in Figure 19. **Never connect an immersion heater to an electrical outlet unless it is submerged in a liquid.** Make sure the thermometer is not touching the immersion heater. When the temperature stops changing, record the water's temperature. **Under adult supervision**, plug the immersion heater into an electrical outlet. After exactly 30 seconds, disconnect the heater but leave it in the water so that all its heat will be transferred to the water. Stir the water and record its temperature when the thermometer reading remains steady.

What was the temperature change of the water (final temperature – initial temperature)? How much heat, in calories, did the heater provide during the 30 seconds it was connected? Remember, a calorie is the heat needed to raise the temperature of one gram of water by one degree Celsius. How many calories of heat are needed to raise the temperature of 100 g of water by one degree? By 10 degrees?

How much heat, in calories, will the heater deliver in one minute?

[FIGURE 19]

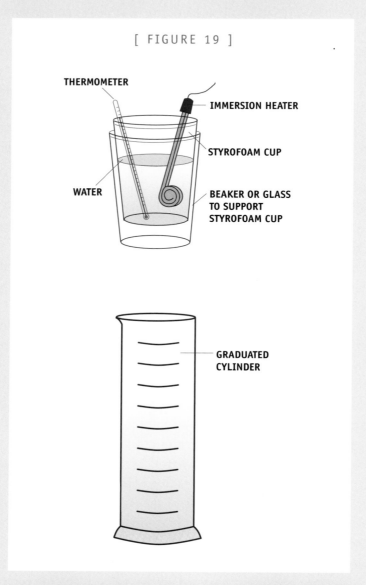

THERMOMETER

IMMERSION HEATER

STYROFOAM CUP

WATER

BEAKER OR GLASS
TO SUPPORT
STYROFOAM CUP

GRADUATED
CYLINDER

A thermometer and cold water can be used to find the
heat delivered by an immersion heater in one minute.

To check your prediction, repeat the experiment, but this time leave the heater connected for exactly 60 seconds. What was the temperature change of the water this time? How much heat, in calories, did the heater deliver in one minute? Why might your measurement of the heat delivered not be exactly the same as your prediction? How is the heat delivered by the immersion heater related to the time it is connected to the electricity?

Repeat the experiment again, but this time use 200 g of cold water. You will need a larger (12-oz) Styrofoam cup for this experiment. Predict the temperature change that the water will undergo when the heater is again connected for exactly 60 seconds. Did the results confirm your prediction?

Predict the temperature change you will find when you heat 300 g of cold water for 60 seconds with the same heater. Predict the temperature change when you heat 300 g of cold water for two minutes with the same heater. Predict the temperature change when you heat 300 g of cold water for three minutes with the same heater.

How do your results compare with your predictions?

Based on your experiments, how much heat, in calories, does your immersion heater deliver per minute? Record this value. You will need it in the experiments that follow.

Materials:

-an adult

-electric immersion heater

-12-oz Styrofoam cups

-glass or beaker

-cold water

-graduated cylinder or metric measuring cup

-safety glasses

-oven gloves

-long sleeves

-alcohol thermometer with Celsius scale (−10°C to 110°C)

-electrical outlet

-stopwatch, or clock or watch with second hand

-pencil

-scissors

-rigid-board insulation

-mineral wool insulation

Because this experiment requires the use of household electricity, it should be done under adult supervision.

It takes a considerable period of time to boil away all of the water in a full pan of water on a stove. A lot of heat has to flow into the water before all of it boils away. Of course, some of the heat is used to warm the water from its initial temperature to the boiling point (100°C, or 212°F), and some of the heat is needed to keep the water at the boiling temperature, because hot water loses heat to the cooler air that surrounds it.

You can estimate the heat of vaporization of water—the heat required to change one gram of liquid water to one gram of gaseous water at the boiling point—by using the immersion heater you used in the previous experiment to boil away some water.

From the previous experiment, you know how much heat the immersion heater delivers per minute. You will need that information for this experiment. Place a 12-oz Styrofoam cup in a glass or beaker. The glass will provide support for the less stable, lightweight Styrofoam. Pour 150 g (150 ml) of cold water into the insulated cup. For reasons of safety, wear safety glasses, oven gloves, and long sleeves while doing this experiment. The water may spatter while boiling.

Place the unconnected immersion heater in the water along with an alcohol thermometer. **Never connect an immersion heater to an electrical outlet unless it is submerged in a liquid.** When the temperature of the water is steady, record the water's temperature. **Under adult supervision,** plug the immersion heater into an electrical outlet and leave it in the water for about 7 or 8 minutes. Once the water is boiling, record its temperature. Why might it boil at a temperature slightly below or above 100°C? After the allotted time, disconnect the heater. By then, a measurable amount of water should have boiled away.

Disconnect the heater at a known time and record the total time the heater was connected to electric power. Remove the heater and carefully pour the remaining hot water into a beaker or measuring cup and then into a graduated cylinder or metric measuring cup. What volume of water remains? How much water boiled away?

From the amount of heat the heater delivers per minute and the time it was connected, how can you calculate the total amount of heat supplied to the water by the heater? How much heat, in calories, was transferred to the water?

Some of the heat transferred to the water was used to warm the 150 g of water from its initial temperature to the boiling temperature. How much

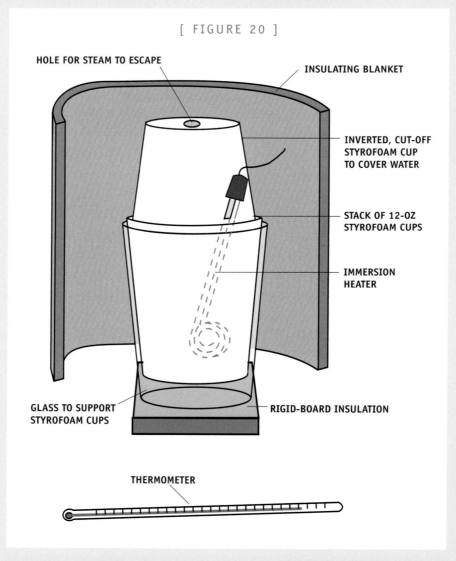

[FIGURE 20]

HOLE FOR STEAM TO ESCAPE

INSULATING BLANKET

INVERTED, CUT-OFF
STYROFOAM CUP
TO COVER WATER

STACK OF 12-OZ
STYROFOAM CUPS

IMMERSION
HEATER

GLASS TO SUPPORT
STYROFOAM CUPS

RIGID-BOARD INSULATION

THERMOMETER

Using better insulation will help you obtain a more accurate value
for the heat of vaporization.

heat, in calories, was needed to raise the water from its initial temperature to its boiling temperature?

Assuming that the rest of the heat was used to change the water from liquid to gas—that is, to separate the molecules of water—how much heat was used to vaporize the water? How much heat was needed to vaporize one gram of water? What is the heat of vaporization of water according to this experiment?

To make a more accurate measurement of the heat of vaporization, you can provide better insulation and cover the water with another Styrofoam cup. Cut away the upper one third of the second cup, and use a pencil to punch a hole in the bottom of that cup, from the inside to the outside. The hole will allow steam to escape. The cover will help insulate the cup and prevent spattering. If possible, use two or three stacked Styrofoam cups to hold the water, place the glass that supports the cups on a piece of rigid-board insulation, and surround the whole apparatus with a blanket of mineral wool insulation, such as that used to insulate the walls of houses (see Figure 20). Be sure you do not cover the top; the steam has to escape.

Using this better-insulated setup to reduce heat losses to the air and to prevent spattering, repeat the experiment. **Remember: Never connect an immersion heater to an electrical outlet unless it is submerged in a liquid. Under adult supervision,** connect the heater for exactly 8 minutes, measure how much of the 150 g of water remains after that time, and again determine the heat of vaporization for water.

A number of carefully conducted experiments show that the heat of vaporization for water is 540 calories per gram. How does this value compare with yours? By what percentage do they differ? Can you explain why your value might be different?

Materials:

- warm water (about 40°C or 100°F)
- graduated cylinder or metric measuring cup
- 6- or 7-oz Styrofoam cups
- alcohol thermometer with Celsius scale (-10°C to 110°C)
- ice cubes
- paper towels

As you know, it takes time for ice to melt. When the temperature of an ice-covered pond, or even an ice cube, reaches 0°C (32°F), the ice does not suddenly turn to water. A considerable amount of heat has to flow into the ice to make all of it melt. Ice melts slowly.

The heat of fusion for water is defined as the quantity of heat needed to melt one gram of ice. Now that you know how to measure heat, you can determine the heat of fusion. To begin, measure out 100 g (100 ml) of warm water at about 40°C (100°F) in a graduated cylinder or metric measuring cup. Pour the water into a 6- or 7-oz Styrofoam cup. Stir the water with an alcohol thermometer and record the initial temperature of the water.

Next, place an ice cube in the warm water. If there is a thin glaze of water on the ice cube, use a paper towel to dry the ice before adding it to the warm water.

Stir the water with the thermometer until the ice is completely melted. Then, determine and record the final temperature of the water.

What temperature change did the 100 g of water undergo as it transferred heat to the melting ice? How much heat, in calories, was lost by the 100 g of water?

To find out how much ice melted, pour the water back into the graduated cylinder. How much more than 100 ml was in the cup after the ice melted? How much ice melted?

Some of the heat lost by the warm water was used to melt the ice, but some of it was needed to warm the melted ice from its melting temperature (0°C, or 32°F) to the final temperature of the water and melted ice. How much heat was needed to warm the melted ice from 0°C to its final temperature? The rest of the heat must have been used to melt the ice. How much of the heat lost by the 100 g of warm water was used to melt the ice? What is the heat of fusion for ice according to your experiment; that is, how much heat was needed to melt one gram of ice?

A number of carefully conducted experiments show that the heat of fusion for ice is 80 calories per gram. How does this value compare with yours? By what percentage do they differ? Can you explain why your value might be different?

4.5 Measuring Specific Heat

Materials:

- an adult
- electric immersion heater
- cooking oil
- refrigerator
- graduated cylinder or metric measuring cup
- 6- or 7-oz styrofoam cups
- glass or beaker
- alcohol thermometer (-10°C to 110°C)
- electrical outlet
- stopwatch, or clock or watch with second hand
- soap and warm water

Because this experiment requires the use of household electricity, it should be done under adult supervision.

The specific heat of a substance is the heat required to raise the temperature of one gram of that substance by one degree Celsius. From that definition, you can see that the specific heat of water is 1.0 cal/g/°C. Most substances have a specific heat that is less than the specific heat of water.

The specific heats of many liquids can be determined using the same immersion heater you used in the previous experiments. For example, you can find the specific heat of cooking oil easily.

In Experiment 4.2, you found the heat that your immersion heater delivers in one minute. You will need the value that you calculated from this experiment. If you do not have that value, go back and perform Experiment 4.2 before you start this one.

Place a bottle of cooking oil in the refrigerator for several hours before you begin this experiment. This will lower the temperature of the oil a few degrees below room temperature and compensate for the heat losses that will occur when the oil is heated above room temperature.

Since the density of cooking oil is approximately 0.90 g/ml, you will need to measure out 111 ml of cooking oil to obtain 100 g of the substance:

$$\frac{100 \text{ g}}{0.90 \text{ g/ml}} = 111 \text{ ml}$$

Measure the cooking oil in a graduated cylinder or metric measuring cup. Pour all of it into a 6- or 7-oz Styrofoam cup supported by a glass or beaker. Place the unconnected immersion heater in the cold oil along with a thermometer. **Never connect an immersion heater to an electrical outlet unless it is submerged in a liquid.** Make sure the thermometer is not touching the immersion heater. When the temperature stops changing, record the oil's temperature. **Under adult supervision**, plug the immersion heater into an electrical outlet. Continue to **hold the immersion heater so that it does not touch the sides of the cup. Because cooking oil is such a poor conductor of heat, the heater will melt a hole through the cup if it touches the Styrofoam.**

After exactly 30 seconds, disconnect the heater but leave it in the oil and use it to stir the liquid. When the temperature of the oil stops rising, record its final temperature. What was the temperature change of the oil (final temperature – initial temperature)?

From a previous experiment, you know how much heat, measured in calories, the heater provides per minute. How much heat, in calories, does it provide in 30 seconds? Since you know how much heat the immersion heater delivers in 30 seconds, you know how much heat, in calories, was delivered to the cooking oil.

The specific heat of the cooking oil is the quantity of heat needed to raise the temperature of one gram of the oil by one degree Celsius. You know how much heat was needed to raise the temperature of 100 g of the oil through whatever temperature change you found and recorded. Suppose you found that the temperature of the oil rose from 10°C to 30°C, a temperature change of 20°C. If your heater delivers 1,200 calories in 30 seconds, then it delivered 12 calories per gram of oil, because

$$1,200 \text{ cal} \div 100 \text{ g} = 12 \text{ cal/g}$$

Each gram of oil underwent a temperature change of 20°C. Therefore, the specific heat of the oil, according to these data, would be

$$12 \text{ cal/g} \div 20°C = 0.60 \text{ cal/g/}°C$$

That is, 0.60 cal is required to raise the temperature of 1.0 g of cooking oil by 1.0°C.

Using your data, what is the specific heat of cooking oil?

Wash the immersion heater in warm soapy water before you put it away. If you would like to find the specific heat of other liquids, such as ethylene glycol, the antifreeze used in car radiators, **check with your adult supervisor.**

4.6 Finding Specific Heat by Mixing

Materials:

- an adult
- graduated cylinder or metric measuring cup
- cooking oil
- 12-oz Styrofoam cups
- refrigerator
- alcohol thermometer (−10°C to 110°C)
- warm water (about 40°C or 100°F)
- safety glasses
- cooking pan
- stove or hot plate
- 6- or 7-oz Styrofoam cups
- steel washers (50g)
- string
- various metals, such as copper, lead, zinc, brass, bronze, or iron (50 g of each)

Another way to find specific heat is to use the method of mixtures. A substance whose specific heat is unknown is thoroughly mixed in a well-insulated container with a substance whose specific heat is known, such as water. If the two substances are at different temperatures, the warmer one will transfer heat to the cooler one until their temperatures are equal. Since the specific heat of one substance is known, the heat gained or lost can be calculated.

heat gained or lost = mass of substance × temperature change × specific heat

Since heat is a form of energy, and energy is never gained or lost, the heat gained or lost by the substance whose specific heat is known must have come from, or gone to, the other substance. Consequently, its specific heat can be calculated.

To see how this works, pour 100 g (111 ml) of cooking oil into a 12-oz Styrofoam cup. Place the cup in a refrigerator for several hours until it cools well below room temperature. After the temperature of the cooking oil reaches the temperature of the refrigerator, record its temperature, but leave it there while you prepare the water.

Pour 100 g (100 ml) of warm tap water at about 40°C (100°F) into another Styrofoam cup. Record the temperature of the water. Then quickly remove the cooking oil from the refrigerator and pour the warm water into the cooking oil. Stir the two liquids thoroughly with the thermometer. Cooking oil does not dissolve in water, so you must keep stirring the two liquids until the temperature stops changing. Record the final temperature of the mixture.

From the data you have collected, you can find the specific heat of the cooking oil. Suppose, for example, your data look like those in the table below.

Substance	Mass (g)	Initial temperature (°C)	Final temperature (°C)	Change in temperature (°C)
water	100	40	29	11
cooking oil	100	7	29	22

The heat lost by the water can be calculated easily:

100 g x 11°C = 1,100 cal

Because energy is conserved, the heat gained by the cooking oil must be 1,100 calories. The heat gained per gram of cooking oil was

$$\textbf{1,100 cal} \div \textbf{100 g} = \textbf{11 cal/g}$$

Each gram of oil underwent a temperature change of 22°C; therefore, the specific heat of the oil, according to these data, would be

$$\textbf{11 cal/g} \div \textbf{22°C} = \textbf{0.5 cal/g/°C}$$

You can use this method to measure the specific heat of solids as well as liquids. For example, you could weigh out 50 g of steel washers and tie them together with a piece of string. Then, **wearing safety glasses and under adult supervision**, lower the washers into a pan of boiling water. As the temperature of the washers rises to 100°C, pour 50 g (50 ml) of cold tap water into a Styrofoam cup. Record the temperature of the boiling water and the cold tap water. *Quickly* remove the hot washers and put them into the cold water. Stir the water and record the final temperature.

The data can be used to find the specific heat of the washers or any other metal whose specific heat you wish to determine. You could, for example, find the specific heat of copper, lead, zinc, brass, bronze, iron, and (if you are rich) silver and gold.

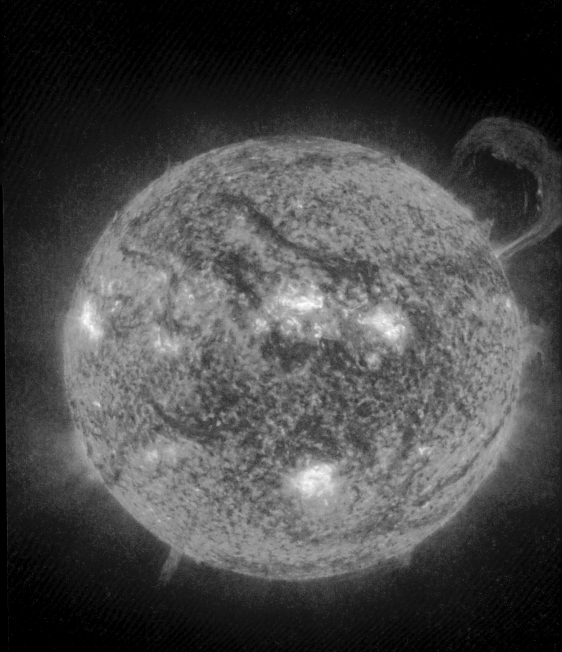

Our sun is 150 million kilometers (93 million miles) away.

Chapter 5

Indirect Measurements and Estimation

IN THE PREVIOUS CHAPTERS, YOU HAVE LEARNED A LOT ABOUT MEASURING AND UNITS, converting between units, finding the volume, area, and mass of different shapes, and determining temperatures of different states of matter. You have made many measurements using instruments commonly used by scientists. But, what about measurements that are not easy or practical to make? For example, you may have read that we are 150,000,000 kilometers from the sun, which has a mass, in kilograms, equal to the number 2 followed by 30 zeros. You may also have heard that it would take 600 sextillion protons to have a mass of 1 gram and 2,000 times as many electrons to have the same mass. Perhaps you have heard, too, that the largest animal to ever live—the blue whale—weighs as much as 200 tons, or that the earliest human ancestor to walk erect lived about 4 million years ago.

These are fascinating numbers, but no one ever weighed a blue whale, a proton or an electron, and certainly not the sun. Nor has anyone ever stretched a measuring tape from the earth to the sun. None of these measurements was made directly. They are all examples of indirect measurements, yet we accept them with as much confidence as you do when you measure your height or weight.

In this chapter, you will learn how to measure things that are not easily measured with the techniques used in earlier chapters. In some cases, you will learn how to estimate the size of very small or very large objects.

Materials:
- this book
- ruler
- dictionary
- novel
- magazine
- paper napkins
- writing or computer paper
- string
- thread
- calculator (optional)

THE THICKNESS OF A SHEET OF PAPER

Using your ruler, you would find it impossible to measure the thickness of one sheet of paper in a book. However, you can measure the thickness of 50 sheets (that's 100 pages because print appears on both sides of a sheet) with a ruler. Based on your measurement of 50 sheets, how can you find the thickness of one sheet? Would your measurement of the thickness of one sheet be more accurate if you measured 100 or 200 sheets?

How does the thickness of one sheet in the book you used above compare with the thickness of one sheet in a dictionary, a novel, or a magazine? How does it compare with the thickness of a paper napkin or a sheet of writing or computer paper?

THE THICKNESS OF A STRING

In theory, you could lay many pieces of string on top of one another until you had a layer that was thick enough to measure. However, such a method is not very practical. What you can do is wrap the string around a ruler so that each winding touches the previous one, as shown in Figure 21. As you wrap a large number of windings of string around the ruler, count each one until you have a width that can be measured accurately.

How can you determine the thickness of the string? How thick is the string? How thick is thread?

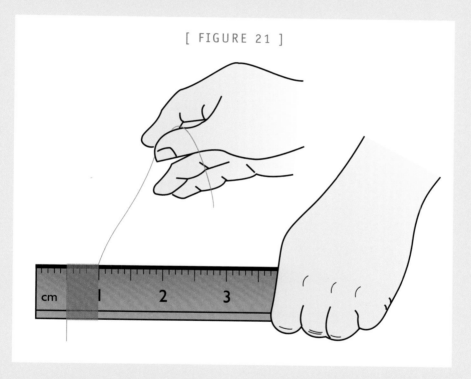

[FIGURE 21]

The width of a piece of string can be measured by wrapping the
string around a ruler many times.

5.2 An Indirect Measuremen

Materials:

- tall tree
- sunny day
- meterstick or yardstick
- sharp pencil and paper
- ruler
- two partners
- tape measure
- square sheet of cardboard about 30 cm (12 in) on a side
- protractor
- tape
- calculator (optional)
- large drinking straw
- pin
- thread
- paper clip
- steel washer, nut, or fishing sinker

Find a tall tree near your home or school or in a park. How tall is the tree? It is probably too difficult or dangerous to climb such a tree carrying a tape measure. And even if you did climb to the top, the limbs would make it difficult to establish a straight vertical distance to measure. You can, however, measure the height of the tree quite accurately, using indirect measurements. Here are two ways to do it. Perhaps you can think of other ways.

THE SHADOW METHOD

If the sun is shining, you can use similar triangles to measure the tree's height. Figure 22a shows you a pair of similar triangles. Triangles *ABC* and

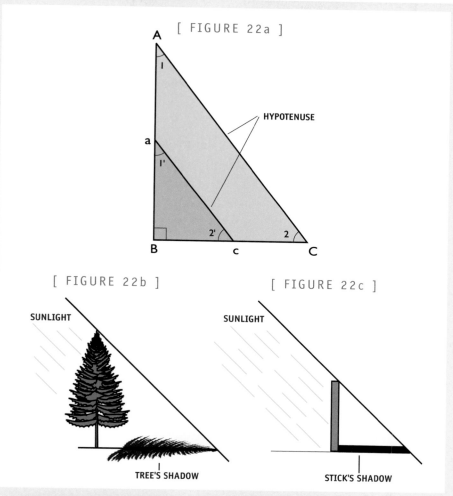

[FIGURE 22a]

A

1

HYPOTENUSE

a

1'

2'   2

B   c   C

[FIGURE 22b]

SUNLIGHT

TREE'S SHADOW

[FIGURE 22c]

SUNLIGHT

STICK'S SHADOW

22a) Similar triangles have equal angles, and their corresponding sides are proportional. The two right triangles *ABC* and *aBc* both have 90-degree angles at *B*, and angles 1 and 1' are equal, as are angles 2 and 2'. Since the angles are equal, the triangles are similar and, therefore, *AB/aB = BC/Bc*, and *AB/aB = AC/ac*.
b, c) A tree and a vertical stick cast shadows. The tree and its shadow form the sides of a right triangle. The sun's light rays form the hypotenuse of the triangle. A similar triangle is formed by the stick, its shadow, and more of the sun's parallel rays.

aBc share a common right angle (90°). Since their hypotenuses are parallel, angles 1 and 1´ must be equal. The total number of degrees in any triangle is 180°; therefore, the third angles (2 and 2´) will be equal, too. The corresponding sides of similar triangles are proportional. If you measure the corresponding sides of triangles *ABC* and *aBc*, you will see that the ratios *AB/aB*, *BC/Bc*, and *AC/ac* are all equal.

A tree's shadow and the length of the shadow of an upright meterstick or yardstick can be used to find the tree's height. Light rays from the sun, which are nearly parallel when they reach the earth, form the hypotenuse of each of the similar triangles shown in Figure 22b. Since the triangles are similar, the ratio of the tree's height to the length of its shadow is the same as the ratio of the meterstick's height to the length of its shadow. Why must both shadows be measured at approximately the same time?

If the length of the meterstick's shadow is 30 centimeters (cm), the stick is 3.33 times as long as its shadow. The height of the tree, therefore, must be 3.33 times the length of its shadow. If the tree's shadow is 6 meters long, the height of the tree is 3.33 x 6 m, or 20 m.

A RATIO METHOD

On a cloudy day, you can use a somewhat less accurate method that is sometimes used by artists. Have a friend stand next to the tree, flagpole, or building that you want to measure, while you stand about 20–50 m (60–170 ft) away. Hold a 30-cm (12-inch) ruler upright at arm's length, as shown in Figure 23. Line up the zero end of the ruler with your friend's feet. Then move a pencil along the ruler with your other hand until it is in line with the top of your friend's head. The length equal to the distance between the end of the ruler and the pencil represents your friend's height as seen from your position. Ask a partner to record that length. Then, from the same position, use the same method to find the length along the ruler that represents the height of the tall object. What is the ratio of the tree's height to your friend's height?

[FIGURE 23]

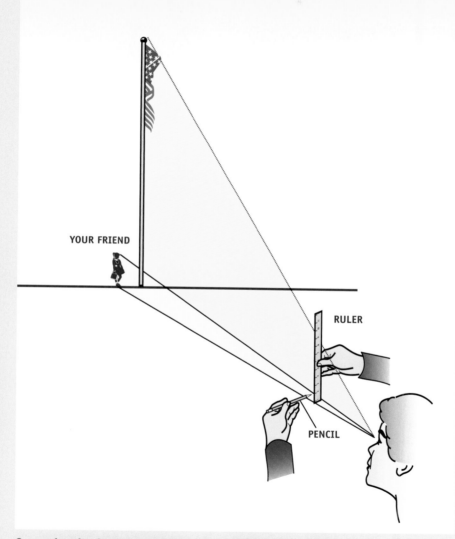

YOUR FRIEND

RULER

PENCIL

On a cloudy day you can find the height of a tall object by finding the ratio of the object's height to the known height of a person or other object next to it.

Measure your friend's height as accurately as possible. You know the ratio of the tree's height to your friend's height. How can you use that ratio and the known height of your friend to find the height of the tree?

Use what you know about circles and a tape measure to find the diameter of the tree's base.

AN ANGULAR METHOD

Having seen how similar triangles can be found with tall objects, sunlight, and shadows, you will probably not be surprised to learn that angles can be used to make indirect measurements.

To measure angles, you will need an astrolabe like the one shown in Figure 24a. You can make an astrolabe from a square sheet of cardboard about 30 cm (12 in) on a side. Using a protractor, mark off angles from 0 to 90 degrees, as shown. Then tape a large-diameter drinking straw to the top of the cardboard. Use a pin to make a hole at the point where all the degree lines meet. Thread a string about 45 cm (18 in) long through the hole. Tie the end of the string to a paper clip to prevent it from slipping back through the hole. To the other end of the string, tie a steel washer, a metal nut, or a fishing sinker. The metal weight and string serve as a plumb line that will always extend down toward the center of the earth.

You can use your astrolabe to measure the height of tall objects such as flagpoles, trees, and buildings. Figure 24b shows how your astrolabe can be used to measure the height of a flagpole. Stand a known distance from the base of the pole. Use the astrolabe to measure the angle that the top of the pole makes to the horizontal at your eye level. Using the angle you have measured and the distance to the vertical flagpole, you can draw a triangle to scale, as shown in Figure 24c. For example, 1 cm on your scale could represent 1 m of distance along the ground. The triangle's base is the scaled distance from the flagpole to the point where you stood to make your measurement with the astrolabe. The triangle's hypotenuse will lie along the angle you

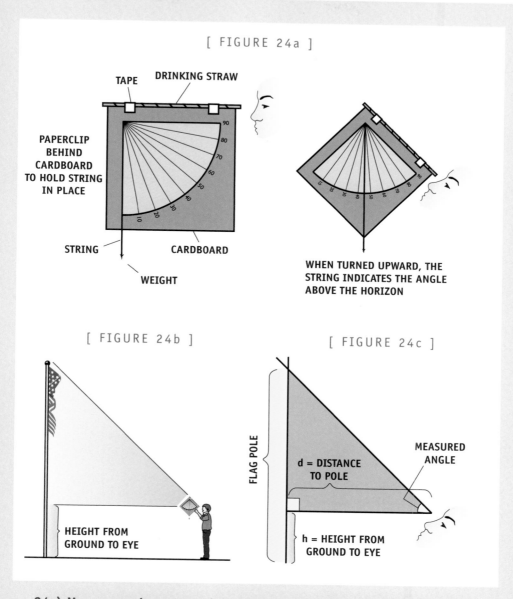

[FIGURE 24a]

TAPE   DRINKING STRAW

PAPERCLIP
BEHIND
CARDBOARD
TO HOLD STRING
IN PLACE

90
80
70
60
50
40
30
20
10

STRING   CARDBOARD

WEIGHT

WHEN TURNED UPWARD, THE
STRING INDICATES THE ANGLE
ABOVE THE HORIZON

[FIGURE 24b]

HEIGHT FROM
GROUND TO EYE

[FIGURE 24c]

FLAG POLE

d = DISTANCE
TO POLE

MEASURED
ANGLE

h = HEIGHT FROM
GROUND TO EYE

24a) You can make an astrolabe that can be used to measure angles.
  b) Use your astrolabe to measure a tall object such as a flagpole.
  c) Make a scale drawing to find the height of the tall object.

measured. The intersection of the hypotenuse and the vertical line representing the flagpole will give you the scaled height of the pole. Simply measure that vertical line to find out how high the pole's top is above your eye. By adding the height of your eye above the ground, you can find the total height of the pole.

Use your astrolabe, a tape measure, a ruler, a pencil, paper, and a protractor to find the height of a number of tall objects.

You can also use your astrolabe to measure the angular height of the moon or stars above the horizon, or the angular separation of stars and other celestial bodies. Why can't you use your astrolabe to measure the distances to stars or planets?

5.3 Using a Known Height to Measure Distance Indirectly

Materials:
- friend or object of a known height
- small object such as a penny, bead, or button
- meterstick or yardstick
- paper and pencil
- playground, school, river or stream, familiar object seen from bedroom window, or other distant objects

In the previous experiment you used a friend's known height to measure the height of a tree. Knowing your friend's height and the ratio of the tree's height to that of your friend, you were able to measure the tree's height indirectly.

You can use that same friend, or any object of a known height, to measure horizontal distance as well. Ask your friend to stand at some point to which you wish to know the distance. It might, for example, be the distance to the opposite side of a river. Move a small object such as a penny, bead, or button along a meterstick or yardstick, one end of which is next to your eye. When the small object appears to have the same height as your distant friend or other object of known height, record the distance of the small object from your eye. Record, also, the height of the small object.

As you can see from Figure 25, the height of the small object, h, and the distance to it, d, form two sides of a right triangle that is similar to a larger right triangle. The sides of the larger triangle are the height of your friend (or other large object of known height), H, and the longer

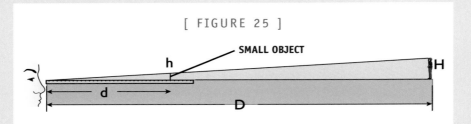

[FIGURE 25]

SMALL OBJECT

h

H

d

D

With a meterstick or yardstick, a small object, and a larger object of known height, you can measure large distances.

distance, *D*, to him or her. Because the triangles are similar, their sides are proportional. Consequently,

$$\frac{h}{d} = \frac{H}{D}$$

Since you know the ratio of *h* to *d* (*h/d*) and the larger height, *H*, of the person or object, you can calculate *D*. For example, if *h* is 1.00 cm, *d* is 75.0 cm, and *H* is 1.50 m, then *D* is 75 times as big as *H*, or 113 m.

Use this method to determine such distances as the length of your play-ground or school, the width of a river or stream, the distance from your bedroom window to a familiar object, the length of a block in your town or city, or some other large distance you would like to measure.

 Science Fair Project Idea

The moon is known to have a diameter of 3,500 km. Use this information together with your meterstick or yardstick and small object to determine the distance to the moon. Repeat your measurement of the distance to the moon at different times of the year. Is the distance between the earth and the moon always the same? How can you tell?

5.4 Scaling: Measuring Long Distances with Maps

Materials:

- an adult
- small washer or bead
- nail or wire such as a paper clip
- marking pen or nail file
- road map with scale
- automobile with odometer

Maps are representations of parts of the earth's surface that have been reduced in size. The reduction is done by scaling. Large distances along the earth's surface are represented by much shorter lengths on a map. Each kilometer or mile of distance on the earth is represented by a much smaller length on the map. Most maps have a diagram showing the scale. For example, a centimeter or an inch on the map could represent a length of 10 kilometers or 10 miles on the earth's surface. Scales commonly used by the U.S. Geological Survey are 1:25,000; 1:50,000; 1:100,000; 1:500,000; 1:1,000,000; and 1:10,000,000. A scale of 1:1,000,000 means that a length of 1 cm on the map represents 1,000,000 cm or 10 km of actual length on the earth.

Architects do the same thing in three dimensions. In preparing a scale model of a skyscraper, they might let 1 mm represent 1 m. Dollhouses are often scale models of real houses.

Similarly, distances can be measured along the earth, using a wheel. You can model this, on a smaller scale. You can use a wheel to measure distances on a road map. To do so, you will need a small wheel. You can make such a wheel from a small washer or bead mounted on a nail or wire.

Make a mark or scratch on the circumference of the wheel so that you can count the number of times it turns as you roll it along the map. You will need to know how many miles or kilometers the wheel covers along the map with each turn. This can be determined by rolling the wheel along the scale found on the map. If a turn of your wheel exceeds the scale on the map, you can extend the scale with a ruler.

Now that you know the distance in kilometers or miles on the map represented by one turn of the wheel, you can predict how many miles you will travel on the next family automobile trip. **Ask an adult** to show you the roads you will follow on the trip. Then roll your wheel along the roads to your destination. Count the number of turns and estimate any fractional turns of the wheel. You should then be able to predict the distance you will travel.

Ask an adult to help you to check your prediction. Record the car's odometer reading at the start of the trip. Record it again at the end of the trip. How does your prediction of the trip's length compare with the difference in odometer readings before and after the trip?

Science Fair Project Idea

Build a three-dimensional scale model of your home or apartment. You might use your home as a model for a dollhouse you could build for a younger sibling, cousin, or friend.

5.5 How Big Is a Raindrop?

Materials:
- baking pan and cover
- baking flour
- rain
- tweezers
- paper
- ruler
- magnifying glass
- waxed paper
- tape
- cardboard
- coffee can
- nylon stocking
- rubber band
- powdered sugar

How big is a raindrop? That was a question asked more than a century ago by W.A. Bentley, a farmer from Jericho, Vermont. You can do experiments similar to his and find the size of raindrops for yourself.

Fill a baking pan with at least 2.5 cm (1 in) of flour. Cover the pan and carry it out into an open area where rain is falling. **Do not go outside during a thunderstorm!** Remove the cover for a few seconds so that raindrops can fall into the flour. The rain will form tiny pellets when they collide with the flour. Cover the pan again and take it inside.

Allow at least an hour for the pellets to dry. Then use tweezers to remove a few dry pellets from the pan. Place the pellets on a clean piece of paper. With a ruler and a magnifier estimate the width of each pellet (probably in mm), as shown in Figure 26. Were the raindrops all the same size? If not, what were the smallest and largest drops that fell into the flour?

[FIGURE 26]

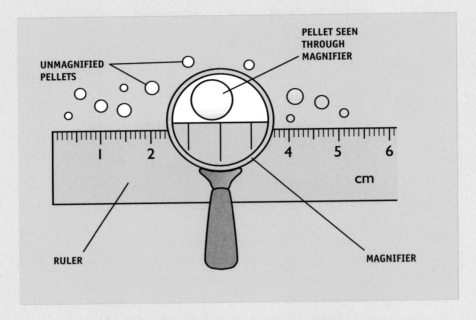

You can measure the diameter of a raindrop. The ruler shown is a centimeter (cm) ruler. Each centimeter is divided into 10 millimeters (mm). One in = 2.54 cm, so a millimeter is about 0.04 (4/100) in.

You can determine the volume of the drops (pellets) as well. The volume of a drop is approximately equal to half the width cubed. That is:

$$\text{Volume} = \frac{1}{2} \text{ (width)}^3 \text{ or}$$
$$\text{Volume} = \frac{1}{2} \text{ (width} \times \text{width} \times \text{width)}$$

For example, if the width of a pellet is 2 mm, its volume is approximately:

$$\text{Volume} = \frac{1}{2} \times (2 \text{ mm})^3 =$$
$$\frac{1}{2} \times (2 \text{ mm} \times 2 \text{ mm} \times 2 \text{ mm}) =$$
$$\frac{1}{2} \times 8 \text{ cubic millimeters (cu mm)} = 4 \text{ cu mm}$$

What was the volume of the largest raindrop you collected? What was the volume of your smallest raindrop?

In a gentle rain where very fine drops are drifting to the ground, you can collect the droplets on a piece of waxed paper taped to a sheet of cardboard (Figure 27). Be sure the drops do not spatter when they land! These drops will form hemispheres (a ball cut in half) on the waxed paper.

[FIGURE 27]

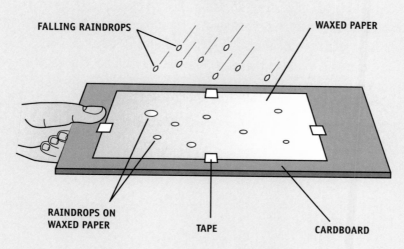

Very small raindrops can be collected on wax paper.

Again, you can take the drops to a covered place, preferably one that is outside where the drops will not evaporate very fast. Measure their widths with a ruler and magnifier. What is the largest drop you can find? What is the smallest drop you can find?

Here, because you are measuring hemi-spheres (half of a sphere), the volume is approximately one quarter of the width cubed. That is:

Volume = ¼(width)^3 or

Volume = ¼ (width $\times$ width $\times$ width)

For example, if the width of a hemisphere is 2 mm, its volume is:

Volume = ¼ (2 mm)^3 =

¼ $\times$ 8 cu mm = 2 cu mm

Here is still another method for measuring the size of raindrops. It was unknown to Bentley because nylon had not been invented when he did his work. Cover the open top of an empty coffee can with a piece of nylon stocking. Hold the nylon in place with a rubber band stretched around the can near its top. Sprinkle a thin layer of powdered sugar on the nylon. Cover the sugar-coated nylon with a sheet of cardboard and take it outside into the rain. Remove the cardboard cover for a couple of seconds so that a few raindrops can fall through the sugar and into the can. The drops will dissolve the sugar leaving measurable circles as they pass through the nylon. Use a ruler and magnifier to measure the diameter of the circles. (A circle's diameter is the width or distance across the circle.) How large were the raindrops? What were their volumes?

Science Fair Project Ideas

- Does the average size of the raindrops change as a storm progresses?
- Are the raindrops that fall in a summer rain larger than those that fall in the winter?
- Are the raindrops that fall during a brief shower larger than those that fall in a long, steady rain?
- How many average-size raindrops are in a snowflake? in a hailstone?

Materials:
- an adult
- box of rice
- balance for weighing
- large log or large piece of lumber
- meterstick or yardstick
- calculator (optional)
- saw
- paper and pencil
- boulder
- large tank of water

MASSES TOO SMALL TO WEIGH

On most balances you probably could not weigh a grain of rice. But, perhaps you can weigh 100 grains or, if not 100, then 1,000 grains. Count out as many grains of rice as you need to get an accurate reading on a balance. Record the number of grains and their total mass. Use the information you have recorded to calculate the average mass of one grain of rice.

MASSES TOO LARGE TO WEIGH

Look for a large log or piece of lumber that is clearly too large to weigh on a balance. Measure the dimensions of the wood and calculate its volume. Then, with permission from whoever owns the log or lumber and under adult supervision, cut off a small sample that can be weighed on a balance.

Measure and weigh the wood sample you have collected, and record all the data. Use your measurements to calculate the volume of the sample. Then divide the mass of the wood by its volume. This will give you the density of the wood; that is, its mass per volume in grams per

cubic centimeter (g/cm^3). The units of density, such as g/cm^3, are a derived unit. They are the combination of the units of two fundamental quantities, mass (g) and length (cm).

If you know the mass of one cubic centimeter, you can calculate the mass of any number of cubic centimeters. Simply multiply the density by the volume. As you can see, the product of these units gives grams (a unit of mass), which is what you want.

$$\frac{g \times \cancel{cm}^3}{\cancel{cm}^3} = g$$

How can you use the information you have collected to find the mass of the large log or piece of lumber? How can you use this method to find the mass of a boulder? How can you use this method to find the mass of water in a large tank?

 Science Fair Project Idea

Atoms and molecules are much too small to weigh on even the most sensitive balance. Yet the masses of these tiny particles can be found in many chemistry and physics textbooks. Do some research to find out how such small masses can be determined by indirect methods.

Materials:
- bicycle
- piece of chalk or marking pen
- long, level path or sidewalk

In Experiments 5.3 and 5.4, distances were measured using indirect means. In this experiment, you will measure distance with your bike. You will determine how far your bicycle travels with each turn of the pedals.

Use your hand to move the bike forward by turning the pedal around five times. Then measure the distance your bike has traveled. How far does the bike move with each pedal turn?

How can you measure distance by counting pedal turns? If you have a bicycle with multiple gears, how does the gear the bike is in affect the distance it travels for each turn of the pedals?

Under what conditions will this method not work?

A bicycle's gear, in gear-inches, is *related* to the distance its wheels travel with each turn of the pedals, but it is not *equal* to that distance. A bicycle's gear-inches is given by the equation

$$\text{gear-inches} = \frac{\text{number of teeth on front sprocket gear}}{\text{number of teeth on rear sprocket gear}} \times \text{wheel diameter (in inches)}$$

You can also find the distance a bicycle travels with each turn of the pedals by multiplying the gear-inches by pi (π), or about 3.14. Explain why the distance the bike travels per pedal turn in a particular gear is equal to π times the gear-inches.

How can you find the distance a bike will travel for any number of turns of the pedals?

Science Fair Project Idea

How can you use number of pedal turns, gear-inches, π, and time to find a bicycle's speed?

APPENDIX:
Conversions Between U.S. Customary and Metric Units

Length

U.S customary unit	Metric measurement of the same length	Metric unit	U.S. customary measurement of the same length
1 inch	2.54 cm or 25.4 mm	1 cm or 10 mm	0.3937 in
1 foot	30.48 cm or 0.3048 m	1 dm or 0.1 m	3.937 in or 0.328 ft
1 yard	91.44 cm or 0.9144 m	1 m or 100 cm	39.37 in or 3.28 ft
1 rod	502.92 cm or 5.0292 m	1 dam or 10 m	32.8 ft or 10.94 yd
1 mile	1,609 m or 1.609 km	1,000 m or 1 km	0.6215 mi or 3,281 ft

Volume

U.S customary unit	Metric measurement of the same volume	Metric unit	U.S. customary measurement of the same volume
1 cubic inch	16.39 cm^3 or 16.39 ml	1 cm^3 or 1 ml	0.061 in^3
1 cubic foot	0.0283 m^3 or 28.3 l	1 dm^3 or 1 l	61 in^3 or 1.06 qt
1 fluid ounce	29.6 ml or 0.0296 l	1 cm^3 or 1 ml	0.061 in^3
1 pint (16 fluid ounces)	473 ml or 0.473 l		
1 quart	0.946 l or 946 cm^3		
1 gallon or 231 in^3	3.785 l		
1 cubic yard	0.7646 m^3 or 764.6 l	1 m^3 or 1,000 l	35.3 ft^3
1 cubic mile	4.17 km^3	1 km^3	0.24 mi^3

Mass

U.S customary unit	Metric measurement of the same mass	Metric measurement	U.S. customary measurement of the same mass
1 grain	64.8 mg	1 mg	0.0154 grain
1 dram	1.772 g or 177.2 mg	1 g or 1,000 mg	0.564 dram
1 ounce	28.35 g or 0.02835 kg	1 g or 1,000 mg	0.0353 ounce
1 pound	453.6 g or 0.4536 kg	1 kg	2.2 pounds
1 ton or 2,000 pounds	0.907 metric tons	1 metric ton or 1,000 kg	2,200 pounds

FURTHER READING

Books

Bochinski, Julianne Blair. *The Complete Workbook for Science Fair Projects.* Hoboken, N.J.: John Wiley and Sons, Inc., 2005.

Frieder, David, and Stephanie Smith. *Get Wise! Mastering Math Skills.* Lawrenceville, N.J.: Thomson Learning Inc., 2002.

Glass, Susan. *Analyze This! Understanding the Scientific Method.* Chicago: Heinemann Library, 2007.

———. *Mapping the World. Volume 2. Observation and Measurement.* Danbury, CT: Grolier Educational, 2002.

Moorman, Thomas. *How to Make Your Science Project Scientific, Revised Edition.* New York: John Wiley & Sons, Inc., 2002.

Wingard-Nelson, Rebecca. *Geometry.* Berkeley Heights, N.J.: Enslow Publishers, Inc., 2009.

Vecchione, Glen. *Blue Ribbon Science Projects*. New York: Sterling Pub. Co., 2005.

INTERNET ADDRESSES

KidSites.com. *Science*. 1997–2008.
  <http://www.kidsites.com/sites-edu/science.htm>

Society for Science and the Public. *Science News for Kids*. 2008.
  <http://www.sciencenewsforkids.org/>

Try Science/New York Hall of Science. *Try Science . . . Home*.
© 1999–2008.
  <http://tryscience.org/experiments/experiments_home.html>

INDEX